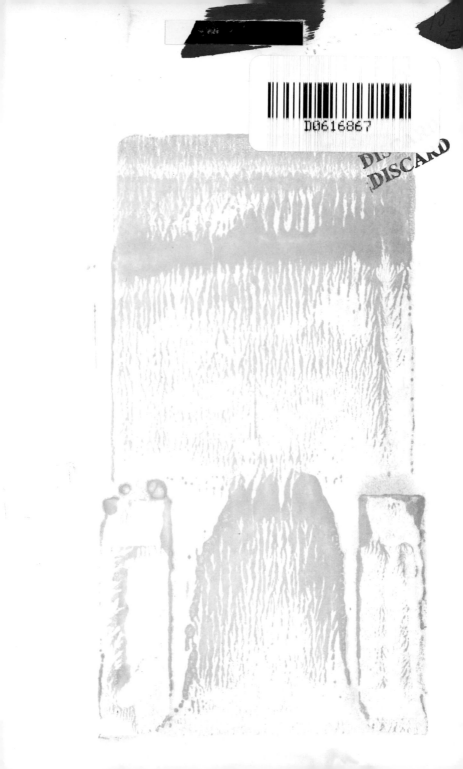

# FIRE UNDER THE ANDES

---

*We must not only have hydrogen in balloons, and steel springs under coaches, but we must have fire under the Andes at the core of the world.*

BOOKS BY ELIZABETH SHEPLEY SERGEANT

| | |
|---|---|
| French Perspectives | 1916 |
| Shadow Shapes | 1920 |
| Fire Under the Andes | 1927 |
| Short As Any Dream | 1929 |
| Willa Cather—A Memoir | 1953 |
| Robert Frost—The Trial by Existence | 1960 |

*Camera Portrait by Bachrach*

# FIRE
# UNDER THE ANDES

*A Group of Literary Portraits*
*by*

ELIZABETH SHEPLEY SERGEANT

---

*We must not only*
*have hydrogen in balloons, and steel*
*springs under couches, but we must have fire*
*under the Andes at the core of*
*the world.*

KENNIKAT PRESS, INC./PORT WASHINGTON, N.Y.

THE fourteen Portraits here reprinted
originated as a series in *The New Republic*, and ten of them have appeared in that
weekly. Two of the collection have appeared in *Harper's Magazine*, one in the
*Century Magazine* and one in *The Nation*. Thanks are due to the several
Editors for their courteous permission to
reprint in this volume.

But my obligation to render thanks does
not stop here; my most earnest collaborators were the relatives, friends, and
professional associates of my fourteen
subjects. Any list of them would cover
several pages. So I must content myself
with offering to each and every one of
these discerning critics my most particular gratitude.

# CONTENTS

I · INTRODUCTION · 3

II · AMY LOWELL · 11

III · ROBERT EDMOND JONES · 35

IV · WILLIAM ALANSON WHITE · 55

V · EUGENE O'NEILL · 81

VI · ELINOR WYLIE · 107

VII · CHARLES TOWNSEND COPELAND · 121

VIII · PAULINE LORD · 145

IX · WILLIAM ALLEN WHITE · 165

X · PAUL ROBESON · 193

XI · ALICE HAMILTON · 213

XII · H. L. MENCKEN · 239

XIII · WILLA CATHER · 261

XIV · ROBERT FROST · 285

XV · OLIVER WENDELL HOLMES · 307

# LIST OF ILLUSTRATIONS

---

AMY LOWELL · FRONTISPIECE

ROBERT EDMOND JONES

WILLIAM ALANSON WHITE

EUGENE O'NEILL

ELINOR WYLIE

CHARLES TOWNSEND COPELAND

PAULINE LORD

WILLIAM ALLEN WHITE

PAUL ROBESON

H. L. MENCKEN

WILLA CATHER

ROBERT FROST

OLIVER WENDELL HOLMES

---

*The portrait of Amy Lowell is by BACHRACH. The portrait of William Allen White is by LOOMIS. The other portraits are by*
E. O. HOPPÉ

# CHAPTER I
## INTRODUCTION

## INTRODUCTION

ONRAD says that all men are guilt-less: it is in that spirit, although I am well aware that it is out of keeping with the sharp biographical method now in fashion, that this group of contemporary American portraits has been written. There are many ways of approaching human beings, and I may as well admit that most of the diverse group here collected are my friends. Some of them were friends before I began. Some became friendly when they discovered that I was not trying to exploit them as "celebrities" but rather, through a sort of identification with them that is, perhaps, more common in a fiction writer than in a biographer, seeking to understand and to present what they were doing and wishing to do on this planet. Some of them urged upon me their relativity in any synthesis of contemporary life. "Copey," for example, that unconventional Harvard professor of literature, exclaimed with true humble-

ness that it was amazing he should appear in the same book with the foremost living dramatist:— he meant Eugene O'Neill.

Why I chose this poet or actress or novelist rather than that; why, among doctors, I selected a psychiatrist and an industrial toxicologist is partly a matter of chance—if there is such a thing —but largely of personal sympathy or interest in currents of American life that have swirled against my own currents. But that some of the portraits are long and others short, some familiar and others more detached, is due, not to chance at all, but to the silent influence of the personality. One cannot present, in miniature, a life of the weight and length of Mr. Justice Holmes's. A subject as complex as that with which Doctor White or Doctor Hamilton has to deal requires space. The poets, of course, quietly insisted on brevity, and who that loves Willa Cather or Robert Frost could speak very personally about them? Who that loves William Allen White—do not confuse the editor of the Emporia *Gazette* with the Director of St. Elizabeth's Hospital— could avoid intimacies or write of the pioneer middle west other than garrulously?

In the beginning it was my hope to have a larger range of professions. My fancy had played with the idea of an architect of high buildings (I do not know a single one), a big business man, a musician. But in the end books write themselves and I discovered, to my amusement, that I had assembled a group that—save for the stage artists —were all of my own craft. Holmes is a great jurist but he has made his ideas prevail by converting them into telling phrase. The two doctors, in their rôle of scientists, have had to write in order to spread knowledge on which they stake their lives.

But my subjects have a fascination for me that goes deeper than my own interest in the art of writing. They are all fighters, Americans in conflict with something—with the age, with evil or ignorance, as they see it—with themselves, if they are artists. Below that conflict lies the fire which gives them their motive force and makes them significant to a disaffected New Englander. Not one of my fourteen friends wears an air of bland satisfaction. Not one has milk in his veins. Here the world is, here we all are; what are we going to do about it? Take something out of life, like coupons cut at the bank, or put something in? It is not only Elinor Wylie, in this assemblage, who keeps a blooded steed, all ready for a foray.

Conceive the group, if you can, as invited to a top floor near the East River in New York, for a rather Bohemian but nevertheless New England repast—call it a Thanksgiving dinner given by an appreciative listener. Amy Lowell, who died

after the book was begun, just before her own
chapter was to be written, but who still lives
for me, would be sitting on my ancestral Colonial
sofa—it shows, I swear, a depression in its seat
that I can never bear to submit to the uphol-
sterer—with her devotee, Bobby Jones, by her side.
Doctor White would be standing near. For was
it not Jones, the mystic, who told me that I
should enjoy St. Elizabeth's and find the doctor
and his wife "a pair of ducks"? Eugene O'Neill
and Doctor White would be discussing the hidden
psychological meanings of *The Great God Brown*,
and Elinor Wylie, just because she has avoided
modern psychology, would show as much elusive
curiosity as she could conceal. With Copey at her
elbow she could always plunge into the life of
Shelley or explore the coast of Maine, and I think
they would go into a corner with Shelley's poems
and *The Orphan Angel* and Copey would come
back with an autographed copy—and hurry to
find Pauline Lord, who in her early youth was
compared with Mrs. Fiske. William Allen White
and Alice Hamilton would corner Paul Robeson,
and Mencken, a little surprised at the gathering in
which he found himself, would play Punchinello
to White's Falstaff and quarrel with Willa Cather:
a novelist he did much to elucidate, in the days
before he lost his interest in novels and she grew
famous with *One of Ours*. Willa Cather and Frost

always talk quietly together if they can, and Mr. Justice Holmes, that most remarkable and delightful figure of our age, would take a generous, sceptical look at the whole company and make either for Mencken, "a clever feller," or for a New England poet with a sense of perfection, an ability to use the material he found at hand, and a gleam of Pan humour curving his lips and puffing his cheeks.

But now suppose that a little Italian boy called Attilio came to the door rather shyly and announced with some alarm that a lot of mysterious saddle-horses were in the street, three flights down, kicking up the pavement with their restive feet. Would not my guests disappear before I could say Jack Robinson? Off to the Andes—off to the theatre, the concert hall, the hospital, the court room, the quiet study where fire burns no less surely than at the core of the world.

Left alone, I should not be disconsolate, only a little regretful that one cannot tell all one knows of living people, who have a right to their privacies. Willa Cather said, after reading the portrait of Amy Lowell: "We should all have died for you." Thank heaven they did not; for is not contemporary life, with its smooth top layers and all those secrecies that lie below, the true and extraordinary romance? The New England sage whom I quote on my title-page has again expressed

7

my attitude: "I call my thoughts the present age because I use no will in the matter, but honestly record such impressions as things make. So transform I myself into a dial, and my shadow will tell where the sun is."

# CHAPTER II
## AMY LOWELL
*Memory Sketch for a Biographer*

## AMY LOWELL

*Memory Sketch for a Biographer*

HAT Amy Lowell's creative spirit occupied a large and unwieldy body is important because the triumph lay with the spirit. Her handsome head, unflinching in its carriage, had much to reckon with. First, perhaps, a passionate and untrammelled heart. Next, physical illness, disability, and a kind of fleshly discomfort that no woman could bear in youth without suffering self-consciousness, and the sense of a lost paradise. Yet I doubt if I have known a maturity as full-flavoured and wholly sustaining as Amy Lowell's. Every twisted strand, every quirk in her destiny which earlier challenged normality and happiness, became woven into the warp and woof of a noble and dedicated career. There was at last nothing she would have altered if she could, even her mortal shape. It was, you may be sure, her own keen, not too charitable eyes which, looking down through her glasses on a figure they could not admire, decreed that it should be encased in a trim uniform of rich dark satin, with stiff boned collar and undersleeves of net, and that it should become, with all its limitations, an adornment and enhancement of that great personage, Amy Lowell.

The high, square, mansard-roofed, brown stone mansion where this poet was born, and where— *mirabile dictu* (for what other American author can claim such stability?)—she lived and died, might again, like her body, have been a prison rather than a principality, but for the exuberance of her vitality and the determination of her will. Embowered in old trees and lawns and gardens in the more manorial part of Brookline, Sevenels was a very monument of security, financial, social, traditional. The woman who inherited these slippery floors, this high-ceiled Victorian spaciousness and ease, had no need save of inward impulse to watch night fade into day through the jalousies of long French windows, with only a black cat for company, as she scratched crooked lines on yellow paper. What Amy Lowell's world expected of her was the enjoyment of an easy conformity, and when, instead, she began to batter her tough and individual intention upon thick walls of prejudice; when, straining against Bostonian precedent, she not only made friends with actresses, and gave plays on Sunday afternoons, but actually published "free" verse in the *Atlantic Monthly,* her career and aims were taken as a sort of eccentric scandal. It was not until her poetic leadership was acclaimed from continent to continent that she became a jewel in the crown of a great Massachusetts family.

Those who have conquered poverty and obscurity in the service of an art cannot perhaps measure the fortitude of those who conquer riches, cushions, and conventions to the same end. Amy Lowell had endurance as well as hardihood. She could count, and did, on the strength of her backbone. Undoubtedly there were many stresses that she could never know, and one misses the trace of them in her poetry. However revolutionary her rhythms, her politics remained solid Republican, and she kept—wished to keep—many of the privileges and superiorities of a social group that prided itself on birth, breeding, learning, civic power and worldly substance. Yet when one drove up to the fine portal of Sevenels, in the green gloom of a summer evening, it was never to dine with the cousin of James Russell Lowell, or with the sister of the President of Harvard University, or, if one were a friend, to pay tribute to a celebrity. When the smiling Timothy had opened the door of the car and rung the polished silver bell, and one had entered that vast antlered hall, and sat down in the formal drawing-room where flowers and paintings bloomed in a soft light, it was always with the sense that this was the abode of an artist. A spirit that transcended the luxury and formality that the eye declared brooded over the scene. It was a zestful spirit, spontaneous, vitalizing, and suddenly it took shape in a voice. A voice high-pitched in timbre as the roof it emerged from, sonorously hallooing, summoning one up two flights of stairs to share the mystery of the bedchamber.

For Amy Lowell chose to wake and sleep not in the high-ceiled, *piano nobile* part of her house, but on that more informal level above, that rookery under the slated eaves where she could more easily perform her conjuring trick of turning midnight to morn and morn to midnight, and by another special prescription, accord the most insistent telephone bell with the most abysmal silence. Here, too, kimonos and typewriters, secretaries and—in their time—Scotch sheep-dogs, maids and visitors, breakfasts and lunches, fires and electric fans, manuscripts and bandages, keen-pointed pencils and blunt-pointed cigars, could be mingled in that highly organized confusion and bustle which were the spice of a poet's more executive hours. Her wide, low bedroom, opening off a wide, low hall, and bursting with books like all the rest of the house, was the centre of her kingdom and her wide, low bed was the very nucleus of this cen-

tral cell; it had exactly sixteen pillows and was
sunned and cooled by a couple of dormer-win-
dows overlooking the sunken garden where, in
summer, fireflies were sometimes seen to light
their lamps along the cone-like, clipped ever-
greens before she left it for a dinner late and ever
later. I have seen her reading in that bed under a
black umbrella in the bright light of mid-after-
noon, smoking, of course, the equally black cigar;
I have seen her "making" it—as she did always
with her own hands—at one a. m., the faithful
Irish maid whom she adored and abused, standing
by to plump the pillows. Amy Lowell's hands
were small and covered with sparkling rings.
Fingers without emeralds and diamonds seemed
to her undressed, almost indecorous.

Yet I loved her best in her unpanoplied moments, without her rings, without her pompadour
and topknot, her hair in a little flat twist, her innocent blue dressing-gown, the style of which
must have been determined at the age of sixteen,
enhancing the blue candour of her walls, with
their bluer Hiroshigis. Her face at such moments
was candid too; Amy Lowell *en déshabillé* was a
New England vestal, despite the colossal tiled
bath-room that marked her a sybaritic empress,
and the manuscript volumes, neatly typed by the
secretaries, that piled themselves on the mahogany
centre-table to mark her a genius; despite the

stream of command, vituperation, and imperious affection—redeemed all three from portentousness or sting by the flashes of Johnsonian humour and the warm radiation that carried them—that poured forth as the servitors and friends who ever accompanied her performed, under her vigilant eye, the detail of her ritual. Ritual and retinue were dear. But, knowing sickness better than her doctor, she must know her household better than her domestics. On winter evenings one used to hear the name of her furnace—"Matilda." Matilda had a very worthy attendant. But suddenly the hostess would arise from her arm-chair in a cloud of cigar smoke and pad down cellar like a man to regulate the draft.

For Amy Lowell was a New England autocrat of the old school, one of those who, having a finger in every pie, make life stir about them, and instinctively take the foremost place. No Puritan, however, if Puritans are neutral-tinted. (She herself declared they were the reverse.) She could not help arousing sensation wherever she went—love or hate, curiosity, suspense, drama. She lived dramatically, and opulently, always for spectators, whether at home or abroad: taking her seat in the front row of a theatre, accompanied by a friend with a footstool and the turning of a hundred heads; delivering a lecture, invariably by the light of her own extra-watt electric lamp; merely dictating a letter, or ordering a meal.

Her arrival at a hotel, as for instance at that high corner suite at the Hotel Belmont, in New York, where she stopped several times a year, was melodrama itself. Like a galvanic shock, the news travelled. Even the engineers and electricians, in their cave-like retreats, somewhere below the subway, stood lined up for the nocturnal attack and the sizeable tip of a poet both regal and fraternal. As for the eighth floor, it was all in commotion. In half an hour, every large mirror in the suite was swathed in black, every clock stopped, and woe to the waiter who did not produce ten pitchers of ice water in a twinkling, and begin to sharpen his steel dinner knives. Woe to the housekeeper who had not prepared the soft old linen, and the sixteen plump pillows. (Amy Lowell has been seen at two in the morning, in a black broadcloth dress as covered with down as a baby bird, relentlessly stuffing feathers from one into another.)

Woe, too, to the switch-board operator who was inattentive in the small hours. The telephone was to this poet, as the editors of the magazines well realized, one of the necessities of existence. It signified the direct word. She could not endure delay, even on unimportant questions, and long-distance calls were the spice of her nights. How often were her New York friends roused from their beauty sleep by a hearty voice, punctuated with brahminical security: "Oh, did I wake you? I'm so sorry—" plunging into some literary controversy or inviting them to a play next week! None of your solemn high-brow plays. She liked them as little as she liked serious novels. Nothing on earth would have persuaded her to sit through *Desire Under the Elms*. Detective stories and light comedies were her antidote to poetry.

Yet she had more than a superficial interest in the drama. It is not an accident that the two human beings who most profoundly influenced Amy Lowell's artistic and human destiny— Eleonora Duse and Ada Russell, the devoted and charming friend, now her literary executor, whose advent at Sevenels marked the turn of her career—belonged both to the stage. The poet might, she often said, have been an actress herself, or a playwright. One of her publishers attributed to her the "publicity sense," not of a generation but of a century. In any case she had a genius for catching the public eye, quite as marked as her gifts as a writer. This is the keynote of her outward career, her rôle of standard-bearer for Imagism, her extraordinary brilliance as a reader, her wit as an entertainer. There is no doubt that it was she more than anyone else who put the "new poetry" "on the map," and restored the profession of poet to respectability, even to romance, in these United States. She could by sheer dynamic attraction draw a mammoth audience anywhere, any time, to listen to verse whose subtleties only the initiate could possibly understand.

Yet—to return to Sevenels, as Amy Lowell always did with a sigh of pleasure—here was a woman seemingly made for a public rôle, a prima donna if ever there was one, conditioned both by her physique and by the serious pursuit of an art to lead a quasi-cloistered life; and, what is more, elaborately protected by circumstance and by the peculiar habit she had ordained for herself from the varied human contacts and adaptations that release and drain the energies and emotions of those of us who get up in the morning, swallow our food as it comes, and fit our lives and work into a precarious universe. Even in that great old house which became a true extension of herself, as necessary to her as the shell to the turtle, she began to write when others retire to rest, went to bed as early birds arise, sleeping the morning away, breakfasting at two or three in the afternoon, delving with her secretaries till dark on that fabulous poetic correspondence which she carried on like a great business concern, slowly dressing for a formal dinner, and beginning the day's work again at eleven or midnight.

A thoroughly self-determined and self-conscious existence, like that, if one is to believe the stories, of M. Marcel Proust. The world Amy Lowell lived in was in a real sense her own creation, a work of art. A considerable measure of its accident, suspense, danger, and difficulty had then to be fabricated out of her overplus, by mental or vicarious or fantastic means. No wonder she attached such intense possessive value to every fragment of it, material and human. At Sevenels, as in a palace, there could be no insignificant acts; none that, worked upon by a vigorous imagination, did not hold the potentialities of a scene or a climax; none that had not gathered to themselves a kind of ceremonial. Nor could there be any insignificant objects of art or use. Bountiful though she was in giving, it was, for example, a point of pride with her never to loan a book from her fine library; those who wished to read her volumes must come to Brookline.

In the realm of the affections the same laws held. Sympathetic to overflowing, tenderly solicitous for friends, servants, dependents, especially when they were ill, she would have liked to be to them the fount and source of all blessings. It was unthinkable that their lives should revolve in individual orbits, that they should choose their own doctors, take their own vacations, live in cities where she was not. Her real predilection, she declared, was for a society of slaves. Lacking that, she managed to enslave, not by ignoble means but with bonds of solid affection, all those whose lives touched hers: editors, publishers, reviewers, columnists; cooks, waiters, chauffeurs; human beings who brought stimulus and solace to her leisure, power to her various strenuous pursuits; masculine peers and feminine rivals in the fields of poetry, criticism, book collecting; and all the hosts of youth. And the bond once forged was strong, occasionally restricting to the stride of the independent, hampering to Amy Lowell herself. For the tyrannous one was the greatest of all the slaves, where a tie of affection was in question. Take the case of the seven Scotch sheep-dogs. Who can forget their seven ceremonial bowls of exquisite food, brought into the library after a *dîner intime*, set each in its exactly appointed spot on the shiny floor or the rugs, while evening frocks were spread with bath towels against snuffing black noses. Well, between their scheme of dietetics, their devourings of timid minor poets—who modestly arrived afoot, instead of letting themselves be fetched in the maroon car—and their ardent devotion, their owner was at last brought to a choice: sheep-dogs or poetry? It was almost a relief when under the war régime the darlings sickened and died.

Yet she was a loyal friend and true, who respected and wanted strong characters about her —not just cushions for her ease—and got them, too. It is exciting to live in the neighbourhood of gunpowder when you are not afraid of it. She valued her intimates for themselves, and also, objectively, for their achievements, and gave them, if they were writers or actors or musicians—the types of artists she best understood—a more genuine and generous meed of criticism and appreciation than they could hope to find on any other hearth in the country. How often did she dedicate her precious night-watches to reading and commenting upon the verses of some young gentleman in or out of college, some poetic duckling who might or might not turn into a swan! She was openly and honestly "jealous" of women whose literary gifts she respected, yet this emotion was with her no canker in the heart of social intercourse. Being openly expressed in a poem or a phrase—for Amy Lowell knew no inhibitions —it transformed itself frequently into a tribute of hearty admiration.

The ceremonials of the great square dining-room, to which one descended with Mrs. Russell an hour after dinner had been announced, but well before the rites of the upper floor had been completed, resolved many a literary dispute. If dignity and æsthetic charm reigned here below, so also did a kind of warmth and ease and freedom that lifted the guest as on a floating cloud on a halcyon day. When, half way through the long perfection of the meal, the hostess appeared, now cap-à-pie, dressed in her fine dark-green, full of capacious humour and hearty appetite, she was usually, to be sure, ready to demolish in talk the most distinguished adversary. If necessary, she would, metaphorically speaking, shake him to quiescence, with queer jerks of the head, like a terrier with its prey. She could be ruthless, especially in those earlier years when both she and the movement she was sponsoring were on the defensive. If her tremendous drive encountered an obstacle that drove it back upon itself, she was dangerous as a tidal wave in her destructive force. But by the time she became, as I think she did, the most arresting and conspicuous figure among American authors, she brought even to controversy the amenity of assurance. Then that forthright, buccaneering maleness of hers, that eighteenth-century gusto for meeting and defeating others in talk, that fecund interest in books and scholarship and the craft of letters, that hardy curiosity about "Men, Women and Ghosts" came into its real rights, and made an evening at her house memorable and rich among literary and human adventures.

I have only to stare into the crystal of memory to see again that beloved Amy Lowell world, which has now vanished away, forming itself before my eyes in the sort of free, shifting, kaleidoscopic pictures of which she herself was such a past-master and conjurer. Here is an outside terrace, starred with purple bougainvillea, above a gentle slope descending to a garden full, like a bowl, of dim splashed colours, summer mist, glints of fire. A young poet and a scholar are talking of Coleridge. A poetess is performing, with humorous absorption, the ritual of the gold-fish. Their diet, too, was overlooked by their god, and how fascinated was an Imagist by the hungry nosings and translucent tremors of the fish! Remember "An Aquarium":

> Slow up-shifts,
> Lazy convolutions:
> Then a sudden swift straightening
> And darting below.

But the crystal does not hold long any outdoor picture. Amy Lowell scarcely belonged even in her own garden, among poppies and blue salvia. Though her poetry is so largely visual, reflects so many forms and colours of The Floating World

(how happy her titles were, by the way!) though
for her, as for Keats, forgetfulness of a "harassing
personality" had come from "living in the eye
alone," she possessed, as she points out that Keats
did, the power of "swift registration of images."
A very little of the spectacle went a long way.
One literary visit to England served her where
others need many. One page of Chinese poetry or
Indian folklore was a substitute for an actual
paysage or a night by a tepee. "Poetry is seldom
written in the midst of an action or state of being.
Reflection is its essence; it is the perfume of something that has been but is not." And so Amy
Lowell, even on a summer evening, loved the
serenity of the great, lamp-lit library, the fire, the
lace curtains shutting out the reality of the sensuous universe, wafting ghost scents of grass and
trees and flowers, which waxing more potent in
the imagination, brought her close and closer to
the creative, indwelling mood of the night to
come.

Now the picture in the crystal sharpens and
deepens. Here are two ladies, facing each other
across a seignorial vastness of hearth. The atmosphere is charged. By the signs, there will be a
"poetry burst" before the small hours have waned.
Meanwhile the striking central figure moves rest-
lessly. Sinks into a great armchair, like a man's.
Cuts her cigar, like a man. Adjusts the lights like

a woman, suspending from every lamp, just so, a little shade with dancing elfin figures. Throws on to the perfection of the hearth those logs split so thin that she could lift and replenish them through the long night. I see a little Constable. A photograph of the Quai des Fleurs. A vista of polished tables, reflecting white flowers. High walls of books. I hear a voice, a full, powerful, resonant voice reading a poem. Perhaps the poem the public later always calls for:

I would be the pink and silver as I ran along the paths,
And he would stumble after,
Bewildered by my laughter.
I should see the sun flashing—

but the voice has died away. What's the matter? A black cat, conscious of his power, has deserted his mistress, jumped on to the orange frock on the sofa. Take care, Mr. Winky! You have a jealous mistress! Ah, the cozener knows his place after all. And as she reads on, all the gleaming surfaces of the distinguished room reflect the vitreous surface of the poetry. Colours and shapes of words, magic words. Colours and shapes of books, magic books. Colours and scents of roses, colour of that sustaining love and understanding on the opposite sofa, warm as ripe fruit, that helped a restless driven creature to fix and crystallize this beauty she is torn by in the shimmer of a poetic pattern.

Eleven o'clock. The spell is broken. A maid with a ceremonial tray. Time for Ada Russell to go to bed. Time for the guest, sheltered in the hospitable comfort of the car, to steal away through the dark shrubbery, thinking of a poetess alone in the library of this great sleeping house, facing at last the stark reality of a great career, with a Mr. Winky stealing in and out. Purr a little, Mr. Winky, rub against her foot. For after all it is no secret that all the dear and solicitous friends in the world, all the hosts of the colleges, male and female, all the lectures and correspondence, the ice water and pillows and black cigars, the great house and American name cannot make a poet. They can help construct a celebrity. But poetry is the creation, as Amy Lowell said, of nerves and muscles, blood and sinews, heart and mind. How easy, if one is a-weary, to lie down on a big soft couch! But no. She sits in a chair, writing, writing through the night.

The poem will not be denied, to refuse to write it would be a greater torture. It tears its way out of the brain, splintering and breaking its passage— And yet to have no poem to write is the worst state of all. Truly a poet's life is not a happy one. Broken and shattered when creating, miserable and void when not creating, urged always to a strain which cannot heal save through immense pain, peaceful only in the occasional consciousness of a tolerable achievement—certainly the poor creature must be born to his calling, for no man would take on such an existence willingly.

"Urged always to a strain that cannot heal"—
that explains Amy Lowell as truly as it does John
Keats; explains the prodigious urge that forced a
woman in most uncertain health to produce between the age of thirty-eight and fifty-one—in
addition to a vast amount of "occasional" work—
some eight volumes of verse besides the one just
posthumously published and those to come; the
two books of criticism; and the two-volume Keats
biography to which she almost literally gave her
life, by allowing her working nights to impinge
more and more seriously on her sleeping days over
a period of years. The report that she died of a
heart broken by unfavourable English reviews
must have caused a great stir in that corner of the
poet's heaven where the fighting spirits assemble.
Yet I can imagine Amy Lowell's saying—"So be
it." Whatever the final verdict of erudition, the
Keats will stand as humanly the most mellow fruit
of her pen. Since she could not shelter Keats at
Sevenels, tend him in his illness with the best
nurses and doctors, straighten out his relation with
Fanny (poor girl), nourish his loneliness and misery with a sympathy like that which made her
own life fortunate and fruitful, she could at least
die for poetry. This Lowell-Keats affair was a
serious one which brought a proud woman closer
than she had ever come to a life shorn of all the
advantages she had drawn in the lottery of fate;

and yet reaping greater rewards than hers, rewards she coveted. Had she lived, her own poetic currents would have deepened.

Her death is like the fall of a dynasty. Here endeth, perhaps, the great New England tradition, the essentially bookish tradition derived more from letters than from life, more from intellectual and social forces than from reality in the raw. The cultural influences of Amy Lowell's day were very much richer, freer, and more complex than those which James Russell Lowell, Emerson, and Longfellow knew. It was during the flush of her productivity that the wholesale invasion of America by foreign literary influences took place. Eclectic and intellectually curious and venturesome, she was in this international movement a pioneer, and any literary appraisal of her will take account of her connections both with the English Imagists and with such modern Frenchmen as Paul Fort, Jammes, de Gourmont. Her art, too, has been sensitive to the modern transfusion from the arts of music and painting, and to certain Renaissance-like forces born of the Great War. This gigantesque upheaval snapped the span of her life into two parts; and though her roots were so firmly planted in the traditional past, she took without seeming effort the stride of the age of Jazz. That is why the young loved her and never found her a prude. She could have shaken hands with Babbit without winking, and he would have thought her, as all men did, a wonderfully good fellow. Yet she was of the lineage of the bluestockings, and she may well be counted in the future with the literary ancestors she repudiated rather than with the new kind of New England poet, the child, probably of a Pole in the Connecticut valley, who will never have entered the Widener Library or heard a symphony concert.

My prayer is that she will find a biographer with as big a heart as her own, who will deal with her honestly, unsentimentally, discerningly, but not at all as Strachey dealt with Florence Nightingale or Nicolson with Byron. It would be very easy for some smart young person to puncture her soap-bubble of fame. But whatever the verdict of posterity on her poetry, whether it be that God made her a poet or that she made herself, she was an outstanding force and influence in the American art of her time; and the really intriguing thing about the odd scheme of her existence is that *it worked*. Amy Lowell accomplished ten times as much in the last fifteen years of her life as the rest of us in a half century, and there was no conflict, I believe, between her aims and pursuits. This was due in a great measure to the unselfish seconding and the stimulus which Mrs. Russell brought. But one never found the poet harassed and grumbling because book collecting and lectures intruded upon composition: she had time and vitality for everything, her public career served her poetic fame, her fame served her lectures, her collecting served her scholarship. They were reversible parts of the same mechanism, and she was as much of an artist in the shifting of the gears as in the manipulation of words and poetic patterns. Had she been as unadapted to the world she lived in as John Keats and most of the other poets of like magnitude, she would have been a lesser personage, less mourned to-day through the length and breadth of America. So let us take her, with gratitude, for what she was.

I think of her caustic, listening face as I saw it last at that table raised above the President of Harvard and other Boston notables at the great dinner given in her honour a few weeks before her sudden death. An indomitable spirit, which had fought the battle for imagism in many obscure corners of our country, was at last enthroned. Here were orchids in silver bowls, here were brahmins in bright array, bringing tribute to a native princess. Amy Lowell was, on her dais, flanked largely by poets and editors: they signified to her mind, I am sure, the victory of her poetic revolution, the triumph of her personal achievement, the sway of the aristocracy of letters she had chosen to enter, over the aristocracy of birth and convention. That was perhaps her greatest triumph, the triumph over her origins. And then she read "Lilacs": her "favourite poem":

Lilacs,
False blue,
White,
Purple,
Colour of lilac,
Your great puffs of flowers
Are everywhere in this my New England. . . .

Heart-leaves of lilac all over New England,
Roots of lilac under all the soil of New England,
Lilac in me because I am New England,
Because my roots are in it,
Because my leaves are of it,
Because my flowers are for it,
Because it is my country
And I speak to it of itself
And sing of it with my own voice
Since certainly it is mine.

# CHAPTER III
# ROBERT EDMOND JONES
*Protean Artist*

ROBERT EDMOND JONES

*Camera Portrait by E. O. Hoppé*

# ROBERT EDMOND JONES

*Protean Artist*

HE revolutionaries of history are more difficult than the traditionalists to reduce to a sculptural shape, or a colour scheme, or even a pattern of words. Robert Edmond Jones, who would no doubt be called a crank in his native New Hampshire vilage, is a kind of parabolic figure in the American theatre of to-day. His sensitive artistic intelligence, so fluid and so versatile, seems to me like the little spotted fire god that I once saw running ahead of the more sombre elder gods in the Shalako ceremonial, in the Indian pueblo of Zuni. So has his talent been the herald of mysteries and changes coming over the hills.

The methods and arts of the new stage-craft are now thoroughly implanted on our soil. Few people stop to remember that it was Jones who first introduced them from Germany and Reinhardt. From the moment when he made the setting for *The Man Who Married a Dumb Wife,*

produced by Granville Barker in 1916, a new æsthetic had established itself, a modernist movement for which he is more responsible than any of his numerous followers or rivals in the field. Not only the Broadway theatre but the "little theatre" and the ballet owe much to his fertilizing touch. He staged the first play ever given in Provincetown, the first Negro plays—those written by Ridgely Torrence and produced by Mrs. Hapgood —given on "white" boards in New York, the first ballet—*Til Eulenspiegel,* for Nijinsky, at the Metropolitan—in which an American wrestled with modern problems of the ballet. Though he seems to spend most of his time weaving iridescent fantasies about the conceptions and performances of others, those who know our theatre best know that in a manner scarcely definable he has made these talents flower and burgeon. As to his own contribution people say: "I don't know what there is in that Jones setting—I don't know that I like it particularly—but there is something about it—a certain extra something—that other thing——"

Yes, Bobby Jones has "that other thing." His otherness is what makes him most valuable, even to a commercial producer.

W HY, then, since he is so much a part of our modernities, do we not see his picture more often in *Vanity Fair?* The truth is that even the intimate friends of this innovator scarcely know how he looks, for his looks, like his personality and his achievement in the theatre, are constantly being formed and reformed out of the mutable substance of the times. If he were wholly an æsthete, as his critics declare, we should see a personage far more crystallized. No, Jones is not "wholly" anything, unless it be a mystic. He likes to talk of the continuous river of light that runs from age to age beneath the changing surface of things. It is accessible to him, and he has to follow its flow.

But you may not catch his mystic-monkish look, unless you happen to hear him utter some religious comment on the theatre like a prayer to his God. You are more likely to meet an honest, simple, practical American in the middle thirties, widely known as Bobby, peering out of hornrimmed spectacles with an air of trustful and effective kindness for his fellows. Or a pallid and limping and exhausted Mephistopheles, lusting for nothing attainable in heaven or hell. Or again a hatchet-faced and melancholy farmer, who has had no luck with his crops. As for R. E. Jones, recently executive director of the Provincetown Theatre, he struck me as a rather attitudinized young man when I met him in the foyer, ruffling his cockscomb of brown hair, dragging his lame leg, pulling his neat tuft of chin beard. When I watched him conduct a rehearsal, the attitude dissolved: here was the devoted chief of a close-knit little family, striving tenderly and whimsically as a father from a recalcitrant child, to draw intuitive truth from the souls of his actors. And the variability is not in this man an ambiguity. Something quintessential lies beneath. As one of his friends put it: "I can never remember Bobby's features, but I can't forget his *expression*."

The "expression" comes subtly but definitely from New England. Robert Frost himself, or Amy Lowell, is not more shrewdly native to the region. No red plush dressing-gown, however Titianesque, no witches' brew of the New Mexico primitive, no European charm and ease, no glass of wine for breakfast, can conceal the origin of his clipped speech, or hide the glint of granite that pierces through the affable and the malleable, the impressionable and the sophisticated, in a personality. You will not know the truth of the æsthete till you have seen him take off his red plush dressing-gown and begin to wash the dishes. Observe that he now has on a white sailor suit—again a disguise, of course; a man of the theatre must have various layers. But he slops about in it as earnestly and merrily as if he had on blue overalls. Behind his easy kindness one is aware of a rather

brittle obliviousness that seems, like his blend of
courage and supersensitiveness, a trait of the theatre. The artist is hell-bent upon his own pursuits.
Like the proverbial Yankee crank, he is forever
tinkering and discovering. But even in an atmosphere where oddity meets flattery instead of the
caustic doubt of farmer Brown, he has kept his
purpose inviolate. "Bobby" is a "character," not
a cult, in theatrical New York. He has a saving
sense of humour, except when hit by a rush of
homesick conscience. I have seen now and then,
moping in a corner, a New Hampshire lad who
feels he ought to be getting in the hay.

The lad grew up in a grim and lonely farm-
house, pumpkin yellow, like the farm-house in
*Desire Under the Elms*. A house full of the forms
and figures of the Old New England, which seem
to have some relation to antique tragedy. Jones
remembers a large and terrible, an almost Lincoln-
esque life in the people he grew up with. He likes
to conjure up his grandmother, proud and dangerous, though he cannot even now repeat her "I'll
lace you as you never was laced" without cringing
to a Jehovah-like wrath. And then there was the
raving boarder, who yelled "Christ" as she played
bridge with the hired man; and the erratic Klon-
dike uncle, and the brilliant medical uncle who,
having lost a patient, ran a saw-mill for the rest

of his life. The memory of this house, with its fine restraint of proportion and its secret, interior drama—the drama of strong, devoted, violent, cross-grained characters, acting itself out in the silences of in-drawn breaths, which, after thirty years of waiting would "let off" something that had been stored in the in-turned hearts—is to Jones more powerfully living than anything he has seen in the wider world. No wonder his settings for *Desire Under the Elms* offended New Englanders of paler and more discreet cast of mind. Jones's New England is, in his own words, "violent, passionate, sensual, sadistic, lifted, heated, frozen, transcendental, Poesque."

Jones—who has a weakness for soothsayers—likes to quote the sibylline remark of Evangeline Adams, the astrologer of Carnegie Hall, that he would, as an artist, "profit by the goods of the dead." For his entrance into the theatre was, to his own thinking, a continuation of that brilliant, fantastic dream where a country boy, with no taste or aptitude for farm pursuits, retreated as a child—retreated to the family bookshelves, for one thing. Here the gods, for his especial delectation, had assembled an illustrated Doré Bible, a Doré *Munchausen*, a Shakspere, a *Divine Comedy*, and several ancient atlases full of diagrams of the constellations. Bobby's eyes roll with fascinated reminiscence as he speaks of them and murmurs:

40

"The moon's my constant mistress——"

Young Robert would have had a hard time but for his mother, a busy housewife and the mother of an obstreperous family, who yet remembered that she had studied to be a concert pianist. Her answer to the plight of her favourite, mooning boy was to project him toward the career she had renounced. She got him a violin, and—though the house was empty of worldly resources—excellent lessons in Boston. See this faded photograph of a weedy high-school boy, in a chin-breaking white collar, who has heard it murmured at the village concerts where he figured that he is not as other boys. Jones admits—for he is a singularly honest person—that he took in the murmur with the satisfaction of a born public character.

Nor was music the only art essential to the theatre that he began to study on the farm. Already he was unconsciously reaching for expression in a direction even more fundamental to him. He was always drawing—no doubt Doré, and the atlases, helped. But it seems that a certain sort of genius, disarming, pure, yet obstinately hard and persistent in its drive, always finds itself protectors. Material for his art dropped into the youth's hands like manna, from casual strangers. When at last, at the age of fourteen, he heard from a visitor from New York that his drawing was "remarkable," that he could "go anywhere";

heard in the glamour of a summer night what Europe and painting were like, his lot was cast. Had he only known, he was half way to Reinhardt at that moment. The six hard-earned years at Harvard—where he gravitated naturally into the college orchestra and then into the Fine Arts Department—the odd episode of window-dressing at a cheap Boston department store, the painful hawking of undesired drawings about New York, were inevitable preliminaries to that mad European plunge which took him to Florence and to Germany.

Two years later, a queer, morbid, disjointed creature, who had reinforced his chin with a flying reddish beard, returned to New York. This El Greco type was unheralded and unimpressive, except to a very select and devoted group who had faith that the disjointed parts would somehow coagulate into a significant talent. And in fact Jones was not long in getting his chance—the chance already noted, to set the *Dumb Wife*. The veiled and pearly sheen of that stage setting lingers in memory like a strange perfume. The first artistic opportunity is not so different from first love and this had something of pure magic in it, something supernal that Jones has never quite attained since. He painted the scenery and cut and fitted the costumes with his own hands.

The success was final and the fortune of a

dreamer was made, so far as Broadway could do it. Arthur Hopkins, the most experimental of commercial producers, promptly adopted Jones as friend, collaborator, and genius of the lamp in the realm of stage production, and when later John Barrymore was added to the combination, it seemed that nothing could stop these three wonder-workers, who flung their jewels at the public in a sort of Renaissance spirit. The achievements of the triumvirate, such as *Richard III, The Jest*—which has lately returned as a tradition—*Hamlet,* are recorded and Jones's contribution of solemn, indeed shattering, notes of beauty is important in the record. It was always a personal gift that he made to the Hopkins productions, even when he was setting airy trifles like *Good Gracious, Annabelle:* the gods had endowed him with a delightful grace and urbanity as well as with the sharply tragic or melodramatic perceptions that seemed to emanate so inevitably from that lonely farm on the New Hampshire hill. Bobby Jones somehow lived always above the splendours of Broadway, he was never caught in their toils. But even his Renaissance backgrounds, like that of *The Jest,* where the personages moved in a superheated atmosphere of mediæval gorgeousness and cruelty, were built with an economy, an austerity of means.

Recall any of his other settings: that of the

43

Carpenter ballet, *The Birthday of the Infanta,*
where lights and glooms and towering shadows
and architectural lines and spaces were designed
to enhance the importance of the exotic little
Velazquez figure descending the steps; that of
Barrymore's *Hamlet,* in which the wavering black
presence of the prince is seen in a *décor* royal yet
abstract, where visual imagery somehow shapes the
pattern of tragic doom. Such "scenery" stands
out in memory almost as an orchestral accompaniment, muted, sonorous, lyrical, as the case may be,
but always with something held back. Stallings
called the *Hamlet* setting "a cathedral of the
mind."

The power of dream abstractly has dangers of
its own, and during his Broadway period the
æsthete dwelt continually in an ivory tower,
drawing inspiration from his own springs, which
bubble up more directly from the unconscious
base than those of most creators. Human beings,
as he admits, were in those days "pieces of paper"
to him, and he was still enveloped in many coat-
ings of New England snow. Undoubtedly he was
moved largely by his own creative urge, and by
his need to experiment in a new and unfamiliar
form when he tumbled into his first and only
cataclysmic failure—*Macbeth.* Here Shakspere's
conception of the dark, elemental forces of evil
was rendered with an almost neurotic spasm, in

terms of the dark forces of the American unconscious that well up under the influence of the
great spaces, the potent heat and primitive white
light of a New Mexican summer. But between this
fantastic fury of modernity and the pedestrian
convention of the actors lay a gulf that no audience could bridge.

The artist had to digest his failure; in the process many of his cerements of ice melted away. He
saw that messages from the unconscious must
be censored before they become popular art. But
he had a more crucial revelation which is still influencing his career, and identifies him with the
theatre of the ages, as distinguished from the glittering temple where so many "scenic artists" are
doomed to perish with their decorations. Simply
this: the theatre cannot be saved by its mise-en-
scène. It is possible to enhance the weight and
glory of a mediocre Shaksperian production or an
empty Italian melodrama, it is possible to lift a
pretty comedy above its own dead level by a
striking or suggestive or distinguished setting.
But in so doing you are imperilling a vital art at
its source. Beauty is not truth in the theatre. But
truth is indubitably beauty, if it be inherent in the
reality and life a play reveals.

In short, Robert Edmond Jones was turning, as
the whole theatre was turning—if in his own mystical way—toward realism, toward life. That

bookish loneliness which had carried a red-bearded El Greco into the fantasy of Broadway was dissolving before plain human needs. But what more than anything else led him to desert the white lights and the esoteric alliance with Hopkins for the dark little streets of Greenwich Village was his friendship with Eugene O'Neill, the most actual as well as the most symbolic talent among our young American dramatists. Those terrible intimacies that O'Neill was whispering across the footlights echoed formidably in Jones's soul. He had discovered, in *Macbeth,* the æsthetic disaster that attends a lack of unity between actors and setting. Now he had the chance to bring both within the circle of a personal and sincere inspiration. His formal alliance with O'Neill and Macgowan at the Provincetown seemed to promise him a freer experimentation with subversive subject matter, a deeper human verity.

And as one saw him limping about his smaller stage and theatre, warming material that was something lumpish with his law of fire, making the minds of his fellow workers "luminous with thought and glowing with affection," one perceived that Jones the human being was, through this humble laboratory experiment, growing to the stature of Jones the artist. "They are so malleable, so unprotected," he would say, marvelling, of his actors. "You can make them anything you

46

like—you can hurt them irreparably—we are all so maimed and scarred." His greatest concern was to help these other souls as vulnerable as his own to reveal themselves naïvely on the stage. "Nothing is so positive and so daring as innocence." "The theatre should be a thing of trombones." Bobby's spontaneous speech has a charm and vivid imagery which recall the talk of William James. How resist a director who feels like "Phaëton, conducting the horses of the sun"? "You remember," says Jones, with one of his sardonic gleams, "that Phaëton fell."

Not all the plays were successful, not all the direction was inspired. But certain productions, notably *Fashion*, and *Patience*, and the O'Neill plays *Desire Under the Elms*, *The Fountain*, *The Great God Brown*, left a unique impression on the spectator. To characterize the impression is as difficult as to describe the director's looks. If the latter are unified by an expression, the plays were unified by an atmosphere. It is not merely that Bobby Jones has a gift for genre—though one must think of him as always in pursuit of such delicious refinements as the ineffable gold and plush piano stool on which Bunthorne sings to the lovesick maidens. No, the *Patience* of the Provincetown was no more the literal *Patience* of Gilbert and Sullivan—if you doubt this, compare it with Winthrop Ames's charming but conventional production of *Iolanthe,* or with Belasco's elaborate *Mikado*—than Strachey's *Queen Victoria* or Maurois' *Ariel* are the literal "dear Queen" or the veritable romantic Shelley. It was *Patience* seen through the eyes of a chimerical young man, who has an original vision, a playful fantasy, and a contagious delight in the material he is dealing with, and who achieves simplicity on the stage at the price of a high degree of sophistication. *Patience* and *Fashion* were probably more complete successes than the O'Neill plays—which is equivalent to saying that these lighter reconstructions out of the past are more malleable and responsive than a realistic-tragic drama to the hand of a director who is also painting a picture, not only behind the actors but with their bodies and souls.

W HEN Jones gets to the point where the bubbles cease to rise in his spirit, when the soothsayers have lost their charm, when he has swung his torch till his arm is tired, and his long clever fingers are weary of guiding their magic pencil, he will sit in a charming room furnished with the favourite *objets d'art* of his intimates and protectors and, with a quaint, bedevilled, memorial expression on his long, pale face, compose his reminiscences, psychoanalytical, theatrical, rustic, and mundane. They will contain many matters of interest, a very gleaming and intelligent composite of our marvellous age.

He will describe, for instance, how he saw birds of gorgeous plumage descending from heaven, and souls of many hues rising like toy balloons into the infinite. He will tell how old Madame Marie, Nijinsky's costume woman, carrying in her tiny hand-bag her total human baggage, tickled his toes to awaken him on the Bar Harbor Express; how Nijinsky tore the expensive necklaces he had designed from the necks of the *ballerine*, and trampled them underfoot; and how God himself, coming to the rescue (as he always does in Bobby's worst plights), took the roof off the theatre and sent a long ray of light slanting on to the stage of *Til Eulenspiegel* to promise a final success. Another chapter, equally spicy, will tell how he tapped the Indian's spring with that hazel wand of his which points where water lies. Another will relate the secret history of the Sky-Scraper ballet. For it had to be Jones collaborating with John Carpenter—it had to be he and no other who first helped the ladies of our most traditional operatic organization to step out, against the clang of the rivets, in a jazzing tune.

The theatre is in such transformation that one cannot forecast what the full maturity of R. E. Jones may bring. It is a fair guess that he will ultimately return to a big stage—perhaps vaster

than any where he has yet projected his mirages.
One can see him doing something remarkable in
the movies—not in the realm of "motion drama,"
which has no interest for him, but through the
mystical medium of the real moving picture. That
is what movies are or should be, he says: pictures
that move. Imagine a picture composed from a
subjective base. Here is a series of images—a girl,
a rose, a knife, and so on—which, as they float
across the screen, throw an audience into a sort
of hypnotic state, immersing every individual in
his own self-created rhapsody or terror, through
the deep-lying instinctive life they touch. It is not
sure that Jones got his idea "across" to the movie
men he addressed, but if you hear his words you
will be lifted into the realm of a new art of vision
that seems to be waiting just round the corner of
the future.

"It is strange," wrote another New England
transcendentalist, "how long our novitiate lasts;
that the period of our mastership still loiters, that
as long as we remain growing and do not inveter-
ate, we are always subject to circumstances and do
not control them. All the chemical agents act
with energy on us, and we come, greenhorns, to
every conversation."

Bobby Jones the man has never "inveterated."
One almost hopes he never will. Innocent and sophisticated, devious and candid, transcendental

and practical, spontaneous and calculating, cynical and saintly, radiant and forlorn, he is that enigmatic creature, a man of the theatre, always moving ahead, and yet not knowing exactly where he is going, though sure as a child that he will some day meet that dream-shadow of all New England idealists, the man of character and mellow human power.

But whatever Robert Jones's human doubts and fears, he is, as an artist of pure form, never in doubt. Study his book of drawings, recall his finest settings, eternally veiled, not too explicit, yet full of an incessant living rush of beauty. Here you have the sublimation of all his powers of vision, feeling, imagination. To Jones, scenery is the resonator of the mystery of human life, transformed into drama. He has tried to render with it such evanescent miracles as the undulations that flow from the garments of Duse or Raquel Meller as they walk across the stage. His settings have often seemed composed for ideal actors, for heroic gestures, and attitudes that have failed to materialize before our eyes. Take the expressionistic *Beyond,* which was a dramatic failure. What we remember is the window over the wide blue world and the fire-lit love scene, and through them see the play as it might have been instead of as it was. Yes, everything Robert Edmond Jones touches, even in this obscure and pragmatic world of the theatre—where by comparison with what is usually called "pure art" all is trial and error, blind groping; at most, quixotic approximation—seems to spring from a source of wonder and brightness. "No one has ever been twice on the same stream," wrote Heraclitus, "for different waters are constantly flowing down; it dissipates its waters, it gathers them again—it approaches and recedes—it overflows and falls."

# CHAPTER IV
# WILLIAM ALANSON WHITE

*Specialist in Human Beings*

WILLIAM ALANSON WHITE

*Camera Portrait by E. O. Hoppé*

# WILLIAM ALANSON WHITE

*Specialist in Human Beings*

OCTOR WHITE has one of those wise, sceptical, perspicacious faces that hold something ever in reserve. It is the glance of the eyes—extraordinarily bright brown eyes, shining out through gold-bowed spectacles —that makes his look arresting. If you went to consult him at St. Elizabeth's Hospital in Washington about some trouble of the human mind that filled you, as a "normal" layman, with fear or bewilderment—about a shell-shocked veteran, or a nurse who has threatened suicide, or a relative who imagined himself Napoleon—you might be surprised to find, in an ordinary executive office, in this United States Government Hospital for the "Insane" a middle-aged, middle-sized, middle-weight, matter-of-fact doctor of sober, scholarly, yet somehow inscrutable mien, taking note with his secretary of some detail of hospital management, like backdoor cleanliness or over-

crowding in the wards. This would be White the administrator, who functions very ably on the practical plane, above that deeper and more philosophic level where he really lives.

The Superintendent would listen to your tense story as calmly as a general practitioner to the story of a digestive upset, grasping its full significance from its symptoms with a mind swift and alert, and expressing, possibly, more interest than sympathy. But before you had said many words you would know that you were talking to a doctor who holds, under his baldish crown fringed with soft grey hair and his high domed forehead, a vast and tolerant understanding of human beings and their vagaries. Here is a physician who is a thinker. It would come to you, in a flash of insight, as he talked, that the cave where the mind of man is located is not so dark and fearsome and unexplored a place as you had imagined. Doctor White would conjure up for you a cavern with well-laid-out paths, signboards, milestones, electric lights, and other marks of civilized exploration. Why not go in, he might inquire, and understand how primitive man lived? The mentally ill are primitives in their way. Psychopathology is no different from any other illness: the pathology of mind, like that of the liver, is just the reverse of health. Doctor White, as he expounds these truths, at once so trite and so new, has the aspect of a watcher on a tower. Though he looks squarely at you, his look comes from within and searches a horizon beyond you.

Is his the detachment of the scientist, the detachment of the confessor? I have sometimes thought that the doctor who divined, intuitively, Lady Macbeth's dread secret might have looked like William Alanson White. Sometimes it seems to me that his bald spot is a symbolic tonsure. He has the priestly aloofness, the priestly quietness that releases itself in the vivid and eloquent exposition of inward thought. The White of the lecture room or the medical congress or the criminal court room is eloquent, and yet a well-poised speaker, reasonable as a lawyer, cautious as a Romanist. It is almost startling that such a conservative personality should be dealing with matters which the average medical man would hold radical. Any radical is subject to attack: when this happens, the doctor's mouth—full and red in the drab of his skin—shows emotion, and the bristling black eyebrows grow unruly and provocative. But a hovering humour is there on guard, casting now a light and now a shadow of awareness. This flicker of alchemy—of something that you cannot quite put your fingers on—is, I suspect, what has made Doctor White eminent and kept him, though clearly a man of peace, on the firing line in the most modern of medical fields.

The psychiatrist, he likes to say, is pursued by three Furies—Ignorance, Superstition, and Fear. These wild-eyed creatures, so much more destructive, for all their bourgeois dress, than his most excited patients, have periodically to be met by a doctor who is also an official of the Department of the Interior in the guise of investigating Congressmen. The Superintendent of St. Elizabeth's was asked, during one of the recent flurries, whether he doped his patients at the full of the moon. I am sure White's reply was cool and patient. He has written that the mind that surveys the world knows more of the world than of itself, and he does not expect much knowledge of mental illness, even from doctors—yet. Modern psychiatry is scarcely fifteen years old. The elder of his neurological brethren are still recalcitrant to the Freudian doctrine and method. I once heard White—rising from beside his stout and Rabelaisian friend and literary collaborator of many years, Doctor Smith Ely Jelliffe—address a group of specialists in nervous and mental diseases on the Language of Schizophrenia (*dementia præcox*).

"The spoken word," he said in his rich, deep voice, and his phrase was terse and effective, "is an ingenious dexterity. Individual experience is largely unique and incommunicable. Yet the world as we see it is communicated by language. The whole interpretation of the psychoses might be thought of in terms of translating the language of the psychotic. We are just beginning to understand its archaic modes of expression, its unconscious symbolism." (Here the old guard of doctors began to bristle. That sentence had a suspicious sound.) "These were formerly considered a mark of mental deterioration. They are better thought of as of a different order of abstraction, an infantile and primitive, rather than an adult order. The truth is *our patients have been telling us what was the matter with them for hundreds of years.* It is we who have lacked the patience and humbleness to listen and understand."

Only a champion of the methods of scientific psychiatry would consider the "ravings" of the so-called insane person worth listening to. Only a champion of the psychoanalytical method would read in his talk the whole history of the race. Doctor White is such a champion. A society that had progressed further than ours in the study of the mind would not allow him to be an executive; it would hold him mobilized for the sole exploration of those fascinating problems of research into the unconscious springs of conduct, in which he is so absorbed. He pursues a new idea with the passion of an Arctic explorer. But psychiatry has some of the harsh as well as the rewarding aspects of Arctic exploration. When Doctor White entered this branch of medicine some thirty-odd years ago, it was a genuinely unexplored field, and his whole professional life—which has been largely coincident with his long direction of St. Elizabeth's—may be thought of as a combat with the elements. This explains why he has always been found at those points where the winds of opposition blow most strong and keen.

It was William Alanson White, for instance, who, under the vicious attack of the "old guard" of psychiatrists, won the day for the acceptance of the revolutionary method of psychoanalysis at the congress of the Medical-Psychological Association, now the American Psychiatric Association, in 1914. Word had been given out that those who supported the theories of Freud were to be baited and punctured once for all. The adverse clans had gathered for the fun. White made the chief defence and did it in so pregnant and measured a fashion that the confidence of the younger generation was completely gained—for the method and for White, who was later elected President of the Association. This was a definitive victory, which has had lasting results.

Another epoch in psychiatric history was marked by White's remarkable testimony in the

Loeb and Leopold case. Here the doctor had a unique opportunity first to make a complete and adequate study of the boys—with his collaborators, Healy and Glueck, he spent several continuous weeks in examining them—then, by bringing the results of the psychoanalytic clinic into the court room, an equally unique chance to "tell a psychiatric story" to the public. Doctor White testified for seven hours without interruption, an unheard of thing in his experience, for the rules of evidence generally stand in the way. Because of the melodramatic nature of popular feeling, because of the violent fears and hatreds aroused by the murder of the Franks boy, he was able to put into general circulation ideas that had before belonged only to the enlightened minority. The man in the street repudiated most of them. But many people hitherto unawakened to "unconscious" tendencies must have begun to ask themselves whether there is not a definite connection between the prevention of crime and the understanding and cure of mental difficulties, and whether both do not depend more on the basic illumination of families and teachers than on the intervention, after the fact, of doctors and judges.

Doctor White's method of relating his life story—which is, as much as that of William Allen

White, the story of a pioneer—has the impersonality of science. He has none of the artist's romantic interest in his own destiny: his importance lies in his association with the development of a great medical specialty. The doctor likes to say that he has been "privileged" to live through the whole constructive period of American psychiatry. When he began the study of mental disease, "insanity"—a term now considered no more descriptive than "fever," or "cough," and never used by the initiate—had a vague and opprobrious meaning. The "insane" were pariahs, shut up in "asylums" to live and die under restraint, and the American specialist in this field was seeking the explanation of mental illness solely in the cortex of the brain, or by the methods of internal medicine. But gradually White has seen these asylums transformed into humane and truly scientific hospitals, where the object and the frequent result of treatment is cure. He has seen the interest of the psychiatric specialist, under the influence of the great European thinkers, transfer itself from physiological to psychological mechanisms, acting without the awareness of the patient.

Kraepelin was the first great modernist: a descriptive psychiatrist, he approached the symptoms of the mentally ill like a sort of observing naturalist. The intimations of Charcot and

Janet were enormously suggestive, but they, in turn, gave ground before the psychoanalytical school. The *Psychoanalytical Review*, started in 1914 by White and Jelliffe, marks the first concerted attack in print of the new psychological ideas upon American practitioners in the mental field. White, by his writings and his work at St. Elizabeth's, has perhaps done more than any other single doctor to get the principles of the new science into general circulation. Gradually psychiatry, this illegitimate child of medicine, has become accredited, even distinguished; taken its place "on all fours," as White puts it, with other medical specialties. "Psychiatry," he says succinctly in his monograph in the Osler Memorial Volume, "is to my mind the first medical specialty which at all adequately approaches the problem of the whole individual, and I may say that that epitomizes its contribution to general medicine."

With this history in mind, White's life, which appears to have no spectacular features, is seen to have a drama of its own. People sometimes ask why he has stayed so long at St. Elizabeth's, a government institution, when he could have made so much more money and fame, and been in many ways more free in private practice. I wonder if it is not really because he would rather live in a hospital than anywhere else, and finds it his best

laboratory? The romance and interest of his childhood were centred in the Long Island Cottage
Hospital in Brooklyn, to which he had the entrée
through a friendship with the son of a surgeon.
His parents lived near by, but his great delight
was to spend his time in the operating rooms,
and he can scarcely remember when he did not
intend to be a doctor. A surgeon it was to be,
then. His circumstances were meagre, but he had a
drive, an intelligence, an ability, and a quiet determination that no circumstances could inhibit.
His talent for teaching and scholarly work, now
so marked, developed in these very early years—
in the high school he began to assist the professor of chemistry, as later on, at Cornell, winning a
scholarship, he became a teacher of anatomy; and
again later, at the Long Island Medical College,
he earned his way by small teaching jobs, like
demonstrations in obstetrics.

Doctor White's approach to medicine to-day is
synthetic, as distinguished from the analytical
approach of the ordinary specialist, who studies
one part of the body as if it had very little connection with any other. White is a *specialist in the
organism as a whole*. "Mental reactions are total
reactions." "The mind is as old as the body."
"The psyche is as old as the soma." These are some
of his aphorisms. He is above all an assimilator and
organizer of ideas, and it is illuminating to follow

back to a very early identification with the philosophical and biological and psychological approach to life his strong tendency to see human beings as wholes; to conceive psychic and physical energy, not as two separate streams, but as manifestations of the same force; to take account, in appraising a psychiatric situation, of the whole past of the organism, including the past of the psyche. This boy, at the age of thirteen, was deep in Herbert Spencer—perhaps the greatest scientific "influence" of his life—and he soon caught up with the British scientist and waited eagerly for his later books as they came out.

Doctor White often quotes, in speeches, a Spencerian sentence that ties up with his adolescence, his internship in a Brooklyn hospital, where social contacts were mixed and gregarious and he discovered young his human tolerance and his human curiosity: "Not only is there 'a soul of good in things evil,' but 'a soul of truth in things erroneous.'" Here you have the germ of the psychoanalytical approach to the patient: an approach that rids itself of all human and moral judgment. The doctor quoted to me also, as joining the young and the mature White, a sentence with which Doctor Schurman of Cornell opened a course when he was a student: "The ideally educated modern man, as distinguished from the humanist of the past, must know a little about everything and everything about something."

Where did White get his bent for specializing, as he began to do in college, in nervous and mental disorders? Perhaps, if he had not been born into the Spencerian age, it would have taken a religious form: the doctor tells me that he was, in adolescence, a faithful attendant at the sermons of Henry Ward Beecher. In any case, his absorption not only in the minds but in the unconscious tendencies of men was definitely revealed long before the age of Freud. The doctor is not a very communicative man, but his secretary produced a letter from his mother, written while White was still a student, to another member of the family, which speaks of "Billy" as "taking a private patient with strange falling fits" (epilepsy). The next sentence is revelatory, considering its early date: "He sits up all night by the patient's bed"—how well I can see him, with his flickering intent look—"and writes down the things he says in his sleep."

White went, a year after his graduation to the mental institution of Binghamton and stayed there until his appointment by Theodore Roosevelt, at the age of thirty-three, as Superintendent of St. Elizabeth's, where he still remains—probably the only Roosevelt appointee, save Mr. Justice Holmes, who survives in Washington. During the

earlier professional years he worked with Boris
Sidis on disassociation, and conceived the idea of
following a word or an association back to its
source, with most illuminating results. "When
Freud came along, I was all ready for him, I had
no resistance to his theories, which I think are as
fundamental to psychology as Darwin's to biol-
ogy." It has been said, by old-line neurologists,
that only those American doctors who came under the personal influence of Freud have accepted
the psychoanalytical technique. White has never
met Freud, much less studied with him: but he
inevitably accepted the method, as developed not
only by Freud but by Jung, Adler, and the rest,
and then proceeded to synthesize it for his own
use in his institution.

The method is the most thorough, individual-
ized, and time-consuming in medicine, and has so
far been largely the privilege of those who could
pay for many full hours of the doctor's time. Yet
White has been able to use it with destitute and
seriously sick people in a public hospital. A poor
old Negress, who calls herself a "firewoman," is
just as worth the listening of the great specialist
as the epileptic was worth the sleep of the eager
young student. Through this absorbed interest,
which White feels and passes on, like some precious serum, to the able young scientists whom he
has known how to gather about him, he has made

a bureau of our government not only a place where the mentally ill are cared for and often cured, but a remarkable laboratory of mental knowledge; certainly one of the leading mental institutions in the country. Kraepelin, himself hostile to psychoanalysis,—even to the extent that it is practised in this big laboratory, where it is only one of the therapeutic agencies used by the doctors—used stronger terms after spending two weeks at St. Elizabeth's. "The father of modern psychiatry" called it the foremost mental institution in the world.

St. Elizabeth's Hospital stands in a fine, high country site, a few miles from the centre of Washington. The grounds are vast; though they contain a sort of hospital city, housing six thousand souls, of whom about forty-five hundred are patients—almost as many people as live in the capital of New Mexico—they are still studded with old trees, and bordered with ravines and sloping fields. The Potomac winds below, and the white monuments of the capital shine out of the misty distance.

When White assumed the direction of the hospital in 1903, it was a thoroughly old-fashioned institution, known as the Government Hospital for the Insane. Now, with Doctor White's new and more humane name—one that will not bring terror or disgrace to the anxious relatives of the Army and Navy patients, to whom so many thousands of letters go out every year, on stamped hospital paper; there are nine hundred veterans of the World War alone—it is a modern institution. Seriously overcrowded to be sure, for the government appropriations do not keep up with the influx of patients from the Services and from the District of Columbia, but well staffed with physicians and nurses to provide individual care. In addition to the mental wards, one finds everything that modern science requires—a pathological laboratory, a medical and surgical hospital, a contagious hospital, cottages for the tuberculous—and besides, everything that a self-sufficing city would need for the amusement and the sustainment of its inhabitants—a moving-picture theatre, workrooms for educational therapy, a bakery, a dairy, and the like. At one edge of the grounds, surrounded by a wall, is a prison for the so-called "criminal insane," which also lies in the Superintendent's jurisdiction.

In an apartment in the oldest building, an ivy-grown brick edifice in the English architectural style, Doctor White has had his home all these years—the janitor of the institution, as he humorously laments, as well as the Superintendent. His study, where Herbert Spencer's works and Fraser's *Golden Bough* are conspicuous on the shelves, is bathed in a deep, rather shadowy quietude. After a taxing morning of work-visits to the wards, hours of dictation and conference in his executive office—the doctor, coming home for lunch with his wife, makes a bee-line for this study, sits down with bent head at his desk, and writes for twenty minutes or half an hour on his book—whatever it may be at the moment. The person who intruded upon that brief pause of concentration and synthesis in the life of a very accessible man would have much to answer for. A scientist who, below his many practical duties and almost tragic responsibilities, lives in a world of discovering thought would scarcely survive, I think, if he did not have this retreat and someone to guard his solitude—as essential to him as to any other writer.

I think, therefore, of White's life as divided into two parts—the inner life of the apartment, which is very like that of a scholar or an artist, unsensational, sober, reflective, creative, and sustained by a central emotion; and the outer life of St. Elizabeth's, which calls on every gift, not only of the physician and scientist, but of the well-rounded and resourceful man of action, who has to "know a little"—indeed a good deal—"about everything"; not only how a great group of sick people should be succoured, and how a staff of forty doctors should be guided, and a large administrative staff taught to deal wisely with mental illness; but how a great plant should be run with economy and efficiency; how anxious and complaining families should be soothed and cheered; how critical politicians, bureaucrats, visiting scientists, Washingtonians needing help in trouble, Army and Navy officials wanting instruction, should have their claims and interests composed. The doctor told me, for instance, of a public official more abusive than intelligent, whose feelings had been hurt because one of the patients had called him names as he passed by. In this institution, Doctor White explained quietly, we use no repressive methods; patients are allowed to relieve their feelings by saying what they like, so long as it does not disturb the other patients. Where, if not here, can they be "crazy"?

One of White's outstanding contributions is his synthesis of hospital routine, in which he manages so to centralize and decentralize that the specialists in any field—be it administration or research—are free to function at their best, with all the facilities they need. As a result he galvanizes his doctors into intense creative activity, and really original scientific work. As I met them in the corridors, or wards, or the excellent library, I rubbed my eyes and wondered if this could be a federal institution, a "bureau" like those others beyond the Potomac where men move sleepily and chafe at a deadening routine. Doctor White maintains a steady flow of young men through the hospital, who give and receive ideas; and unlike most administrators, he never stands in the way of the advancement of his ablest men, but sends them out as apostles of the new wisdom. His influence is to be felt, through his disciples, in every part of our country.

So the picture that one brings away from St. Elizabeth's is painted in the clear colours of hope rather than in the black tones of despair. I have never had so great a sense of the power of the mind as in this hospital where mind is clouded. In the wards, in the grounds, these droves of rather featureless human beings, wandering in their various mazes of thought that has gone astray. But flowing all about them, an electric current of humane, scientific interest and robust youth. The staff of St. Elizabeth's does not hold the patients lost and miserable souls, but human beings like you and me, who can be helped, perhaps altogether cured: whose strange ideas and language have a coherence of their own, like some hieroglyphics that only need the interpretation of the scholar and that have a vital bearing on all normal human life. (One doctor, I remember, was telling the librarian of a thrilling discovery of a likeness between the symbols of the Hopi Indians and those of the schizophrenic.) At St. Elizabeth's the distinctions between mind and body, disease and health, normality and abnormality, mean little. They are, as White would say, "pseudo-problems." Doctor White does not love his patients less than the old-fashioned doctor, but he is in addition fascinated by them: indulgent to them, in the sense of not exercising moral judgments, even about a man who has murdered his wife; ready to listen to "nonsense" because of what it will reveal.

After several days with White, I decided that his true mission in life was the diffusion of veracious knowledge about ourselves. A talk with him makes the average physician seem as secretive as the Indian medicine-man. White has as much to offer the layman as the scientist. He is no more concerned by the poor woman who is nagged by her buried self, or the paranoid patient who believes himself to be Julius Cæsar, or the hysterical child who breaks all her fingers to attract attention to a shame she cannot voice, than by the eminent lawyer who cannot take a subway train because of his fear of crowds, the banker who in spite of superior brain feels inferior to his business associates, the love-lorn bachelor who somehow or other cannot marry. Such impediments to dynamic happiness and accomplishment are symptoms of universal conflicts which lie below the level of consciousness, difficulties fatalistically

accepted as inevitable, until the new psychiatry
came into being.

Psychopathology is highly pertinent to modern
life because it recognizes man as a social animal
and mental disturbance as dislocation of man as
a member of the herd. We can be as crazy as we
like on a desert island and almost as crazy as we
like on a lonely farm, but in New York or Chicago we must adjust ourselves to the complex
civilization we have made or go under altogether.
Therefore White disdains no outlet for his ideas
that leads into community life. The tuberculosis
expert, the judge, the social worker, the voca-
tional adviser, the teacher, the policeman, have
even more to learn from him than the mental expert. He has defectives and delinquents always
under his eye, and believes that the greater proportion of the people in prisons are mental defectives. The criminal should be regarded as an
individual of the primitive or childish order,
whose actions are an anachronism on the adult
level; not as a scapegoat to be punished to satisfy
the unconscious fears and the vengeance motive
of the mob. He needs understanding and often
medical care. In the prison, but not more so than
in the whole institution, the doctor sees the catas-
trophic end of those troubles of social maladjust-
ment in which an ounce of prevention years
earlier—protection for a defective intelligence,

74

understanding on the part of teacher or parent
of the needs of a wayward boy or girl—would
have been worth all the pounds of cure he can
give to-day. "The awakening consciousness of
man in himself is a new instrument of civilization, a new tool for fashioning human destiny."

Certainly if the knowledge already possessed by
St. Elizabeth's of the springs of human lives—
and any doctor of this school would tell you that
it is a mere fragment of what will be available
in twenty years—were really capitalized in the
American community to-day, a goodly proportion of the ills that bring people to St. Elizabeth's
would be done away with. The life of the institution might be thought of as a combination of
crisis and routine. Without crisis, there would be
no revelation of the depths; routine is the means
of adjustment. I saw an efficient girl who directs
the cutting out of two thousand dresses a year in
the receiving pavilion; she was, before she came,
a wild little bandit who enticed men into her car
and then allowed them to be robbed on a country
road. I saw a pretty young girl who seemed to be
the right hand of the nurses; she had been a defective prostitute, hauled out of a "nigger den."
I saw a brutal-looking Negro keeping the hospital
floors in a marvellous state of polish; he has the
mentality of a child of three, but here he is one
hundred per cent efficient. White's object is to

find for everybody the right social level, however restricted. Some of his patients, who turn useful and adequate members of the hospital community, will always need a measure of protection; others will go out into the world again, but infinitely better armed than before.

T HIS, you might say, is the portrait of an institution, not the portrait of a man. William Alanson White is inseparable from his institution, his patients, his ideas about them. Doctor Brill once said that the prime requisite for a psychoanalyst was an inexhaustible interest in human nature. White uses a phrase that a novelist might be equally glad to claim: the psychiatrist is a man who can "feel himself into" another's ways of thinking and feeling. But the novelist can choose his paths of human interest, and the psychiatrist's imagination and his humane charity must be ready to occupy itself with objects that frequently seem unworthy, or repugnant. More and more is White's imagination allured by that biological vision which sees man as "a life-bearing system related with his kind, with all animate creation, with the inorganic constituents of the earth, with the cosmos."

The doctor makes no pretensions to being a great original thinker. But he has the gift, as he sits in that shaded study, of drawing all the threads of his daily life into a synthesis and handing them out again woven into an intelligible and speculative pattern. If he is a great man, it is as a popularizer. When he becomes a teacher—and he is professor of psychiatry in four colleges in the city of Washington: the Jesuit University of Georgetown, George Washington University, and, notably, the Army and Navy Medical Schools—when he becomes a writer—and the bibliography of his works shows that he has been prolific both in a strictly scientific and a relatively popular vein —when he goes into the court room to testify, it is always to carry into the greater world ideas that seem to him fundamental to the progress of man's knowledge of himself. White's influence upon our army, though little known to the layman, has been of great importance. Through his teaching, the regular officer was in the late World War far more able than the physician from civil life to deal adequately and humanely with the mental derangements due to war stress. As to his writings they are not the kind that find favour on the bursting book-counters devoted to the "new psychology." He does not belong to the "miraculous" school: he does not draw his illustrations predominantly from sex; for all his alchemist's head, he does not go in for magic cures. But he employs speculation deliberately to provoke response and criticism. We have to fashion new tools, he says, to penetrate the unknown.

Sir William Osler was a great man in the medicine of his time because, by his combination of rich human qualities and advanced scientific vision, he stood midway between the old empirical doctor and the testubian. So William Alanson White, a much less picturesque figure—a shortish, stoutish, middle-aged man, with a flicker of fire in his impassive, inscrutable face—in another generation and another field of medicine, seems to take his place as sort of midway man between the psychiatrist of the past and the future. On his left is the isolated specialist of twenty years ago, marooned with his "insane" patients on a bleak island inaccessible to medical science; on his right the still shadowy figure of the mental expert of the future, who will, if Doctor White and his kind prevail over the "Three Furies," take his place with the internist at the bed-side of the heart patient, and have a very familiar place in our public and private lives.

# CHAPTER V

# EUGENE O'NEILL

*Man with a Mask*

EUGENE O'NEILL

*Camera Portrait by E. O. Hoppé*

# EUGENE O'NEILL

*Man with a Mask*

UGENE O'NEILL has ever walked alone, and seemed a stranger to those about him. While still unaware who and what he was, he suffered from this isolation and tried to destroy it by putting on a disguise of romantic adventure. In his photographs you will see a mask of arrogant disdain. The tortured dreamer's eyes, the tossed black head, with its streaks of white, the scowling, thunderous face, glimpsed at some formal dress rehearsal, escaping from praise, seem also to confirm the legend. But if you corner the playwright you will find him sorry and uneasy in his aloofness. And it may be that some flash of understanding will bring out, from behind the barrier, with a smile of doubting trust, the sensitive thirteen-year-old boy whom you recognize as O'Neill the poet.

Always thus hiding, always thus revealing himself, this Irish-American mystic, with his strange duality of being, has made his plays a projection of his struggles with the unmanageable universe. Their power and their tension, profoundly felt even by those who resist their implications, are the power of O'Neill's mind and the tension of his taut spirit, which are ever trying, like a pair of acrobats, to transcend themselves. Even the plays that fail to convince as art, or life, have an uncanny way of piercing the spectator in the ribs with some blade of vital truth. Those who are looking for diversion in the theatre cannot endure O'Neill's stark and desperate revelations. Revelation of weakness, fear, cruelty, self-pity, lust, bitterness and revolt of spirit. Revelation of control, tenderness, understanding, love, and a passion for ideal beauty so secret that it has been slow to risk open expression. One used to hear the young sophisticates streaming out of the Provincetown, after *The Hairy Ape,* rejoicing that here at last is a cynical social analyst who does not temporize with brutal fact. Here is our Strindberg. But one has more recently seen the lowbrows, after *The Great God Brown,* swept off their feet by the rush of those hidden tides of feeling which they have just discerned flowing beneath naturalistic surfaces. What will the audiences say when they see that great mystery, *Lazarus Laughed*—a wholly imaginary reconstruction of Lazarus's second life on earth, with a title suggested by the

82

"Jesus wept" of the Gospel story of the miracle—
and recognize that the ironic fatalist has found a
religious faith in life?

"I see Gene," said one of his friends, "in each
new play that, like *Lazarus*, marks a turning-
point, surrounded by a crowd of O'Neills who
represent the skins and the personalities he has
shed." Shed on his road to salvation, he might have
said. For it is salvation the playwright is ever seeking, even when, in *Lazarus*, he gives his biblical
hero an interpretive chorus and a pagan serenity
of acceptation. O'Neill is an agnostic, but an
agnostic in search of redemption. One might trace
his life like one of those dry, south-western roads
where the Penitente Brothers have laid down the
dead man they are carrying. O'Neill's plays, up
to now, are crosses that mark the laying down of
some outworn shell of existence. Follow the road
he travels and you will often hear the sound of
flagellation. Look and you will see that the cruel
whip is brought down by a tormented soul on
his own back. But flowers grow on this desert
track, and the mountains and the sunset lie "beyond the horizon."

You cannot be near O'Neill without recognizing in him a unique temperament with a unique
power of concentration. No Pope was ever more
vowed to his cult than this man of thirty-seven to
his task as an artist. The tension of the strung

bow, which his whole lithe body and physical movement reveals when he is swimming, for instance, as he likes to do every day for several hours, seems like the beauty of his brow and eyes to reflect some inward fixation. His veiled, proud look, which now yields to a kind of haggard discomfort and now to a boyish, grinning intimacy, only half conceals his incandescent imagination, his devouring confident ambition to hit the stars. In spite of that high reputation which he is quite Irish enough to enjoy, in his secret heart—"the foremost American playwright," the "foremost writer of plays in English"—there is nothing crystallized about him. He is a man in a state of growth, a man in a state of progression, a man in a state of effort. His wife, his friends, his dramatic associates, his very days arrange themselves in the pattern which will best protect and fertilize his productivity. Though he still writes to live, in the larger economic sense, far more truly does he live to write. He knows few inhibitions and is never so happy as when he is working. Yet there is not the least suggestion in him of the "literary cuss," or even of the journalist. He has never consciously sought experience as copy, or, like the French *précieux*, "found life an unfortunate impediment to writing." Life has been quintessential and dear to him. What then has caused this passionate flow of himself into his works?

84

The obvious and immediate cause was a sharp blockade which arrested in mid-course his career of raw life and threw him on his back in a tuberculosis sanatorium. His rapid unmeasured movement over the face of the globe had been both a search and an evasion. Condemned to physical immobility, he suddenly came face to face with two men—the O'Neill he really was and the O'Neill he wished to be. Your single-minded nomad, your man of action, may be impeded but is not essentially altered by illness. I once knew an aviator who lay in a sanatorium planning future flights and an explorer who there climbed the Himalyas. O'Neill turned straight inward and bluntly asked himself where he was going. Did he not already hold the universe like an orange in his hand, was it not time to squeeze from it the juice of art—for what other purpose had he been exploring the dark tunnels of human misery, and piling the glories of life to the skies? The answer was that phenomenal outburst of original dramatic work that has produced, in thirteen years, besides many plays destroyed for their imperfections, twenty-four plays. O'Neill never does things by halves. When he drives a car, it must be a high-power machine which devours the miles like air. When he writes, he must try to reduce the mileage of experience by an equally intense velocity of movement.

That the child of a successful and talented actor should write plays seems natural enough. But that the son of James O'Neill, the matinée idol, who made his fifty thousand year after year by playing *The Count of Monte Cristo* across the continent, should have written plays that were not only unsuited to the popular stage of the hour but deliberately proved the hollowness of romance, the impotence of aspiration, the falseness of sentiment, the tendency of life to cheat those who believe in it, this requires some explanation. O'Neill's unconscious life is so close to the surface that it is always appearing as the wrestling antagonist of the conscious. Born to love, rather than to hate, he is so aware of the vulnerability of the ardent lover that he still eyes the world with an almost animal suspicion, as if it would leap at him from behind. Born to the drive of the creative spirit, he has so feared impediment that he still wears, on occasion, the mask of Dion, the unsuccessful creator. Born into security, ease, substance, he long repudiated them for danger, want, and struggle.

Yet this man who in youth passed as a vagabond and a social rebel is, as revealed by his works and his own mature life, deeply bound to that human family which the psychologists find to be the base of our human existence. The themes of the stern father, the sheltering earth mother, the sons who fight for freedom, are, like the theme of marriage itself, too recurrent in the plays not to be referable to personal experience. It was from the fixed family base that O'Neill departed on his wild adventures. It was from the spiritual grip of bonds of which he was unwilling to admit the strength that he was precipitated into those ironic revolts which long dictated the shape and texture of his work. O'Neill started with a twist—the twist of revenge. Life had made him glowing promises. Life failed to keep them. He would pay it back in its own coin for its betrayals.

Lately I saw O'Neill reading the early volumes of Proust. They called up for him, and for those who listened to his halting reminiscence—he speaks rather in pauses than in sentences—a hypersensitive little boy of six, a slight, straight figure, with enormous brown eyes which reflect a shy adoration—a little boy whom Shane, the son of Eugene, must strongly resemble. The lot of the son of James O'Neill was not more enviable than that of most actors' children, though James, being an Irish Catholic, handsome and gifted, had due regard for property and power. He invested his money in Connecticut real estate and chose for his wife a beautiful girl from a convent, who did not accept the stage folk as her equals, and never mingled in her husband's world. But she travelled always with him, and made her existence and her children's subject to her czar.

So life delivered Gene, in the large towns of the country where he spent his first years, to Sarah, an English nurse, who—it is well worth noting— fed him on murder stories from the papers, and for diversion took him to the Chamber of Horrors at the Eden Musée. Then, Sarah and her melodramas vanishing into some dreary New York street, where he spent his briefer holidays, life again delivered him, at seven, to the boarding-school of some Catholic Sisters of Charity, who, when he was thirteen, were succeeded by Christian Brothers. O'Neill has acute memories of the outbursts of hysterical loneliness that overtook him on every return to his rigid Christian exile. Gazing afar upon a stage where a heroic figure strutted, towards a lovely distant mother to whom he stretched his arms in vain, he conceived the world in which he was at mercy of his affections as disastrous, and began to create, in fancy, an exquisite and consoling substitute. No doubt we see an ideal shadow of this fantasy world in such plays as *The Fountain,* in the Chinese scenes in *Marco Millions.* In later years the poet's gift of imagination was to be vital to the playwright. But at this period it served to increase the discrepancy between the vision of the heart and the crass facts of daily living.

Yet the world had to be met: the shy and insufficient school-boy had to come out of his cloister. The plays which outline the diverse natures of two brothers give the key of that deep spiritual duality to which I have referred, suggest what an important rôle a brother played in O'Neill's own initiation into life. In *Beyond the Horizon,* they are the practical man and the dreamer, who love, destroy, and thwart one another. In *Desire Under the Elms,* they are allies, who steal the old man's gold, and make off for California. In *The Great God Brown,* they are two men, a striving creator and a practical Babbitt, two sides of one nature, who must be mutually crucified to fit into one skin. In *Lazarus Laughed,* they are Caligula, the destroyer, and the resurrected hero who has found a faith in the shadow of death. Gene O'Neill also had a beloved brother, Jim, ten years his senior. Jim symbolized hardboiled masculinity and stimulated his revolt against "the old man." Jim was an actor. Jim loved wine, woman, and song; he had easy social graces which a prickly youngster envied and tried to emulate.

O'Neill was subject, deeply subject in adolescence, to another romantic influence, that of books. He read not once but every summer, in his father's house in New London, the fifty volumes of Dumas, the complete works of Victor Hugo and Charles Lever, the Irish romancer. To the pleasure of James O'Neill, who used to harp on the glorious deeds of Shane the Proud and the other O'Neills, he was also an avid reader of Irish history. The romantic poetry of Scott he loved at a very early age and was—this seems important—"a fiend on Byron," reciting *Childe Harold* interminably. He absorbed Dickens and Kipling, and at a somewhat later age Jack London and Conrad, and conceived the idea of becoming himself a Conrad hero, a "super-tramp." At eighteen, spurred by Benjamin Tucker, the famous philosophical anarchist, a thinker who has greatly influenced his "inner self," he read Nietzsche. Between the brother and the books he put on the protective coat of a waster and a wanderer; sought escape over "dat ole davil sea"—the element that seemed at the farthest remove from the successful stage of the paternal autocrat.

During the next years O'Neill was so busy trying to deceive himself that he quite succeeded in deceiving the world. His suspension from Princeton; his life as a sailor and in the countries to which the sea gave access—South America, Honduras; his prospecting for gold; his selling of sewing-machines and his life "on the beach," at Buenos Aires; his life with the down and outs at that New York water-side dive, Jimmy-the-Priest's, where the first scene of *Anna Christie* is laid; his friendship with humble men of all nations, like that Chris Christopherson, also of *Anna Christie*, who froze to death after a drunk; his association with the sailors whom we meet in the one-act plays and *The Hairy Ape*—this has been much exploited. When some day, sitting perhaps by a Maine lake, with Shane pulling in perch off shore, and a well-ordered domestic life in full swing up the hill, he tells you about it, you will find that the mature man rather resents the degree to which his early admirers falsify the tale by stupid invention. The reality was, he says, a thousand times more incredible and imaginative.

If the motive for his *Wanderlust* was romantic, it was tragedy, naked suffering reality that he found; it was insight into the lives of the under dogs of the earth. I have spoken of O'Neill's tendency to fast driving. So had he to drain the bottle to the dregs, so had he to share the worst fate of man. Only when he got so low that there was no further to go, only in the religious and Christlike security of the very bottom, was he at this period free and himself. He will tell you that when, some years later, at the beginning of his playwriting days, he was haunting Greenwich Village, he still sought refuge at the Hell-hole, on lower Sixth Avenue, with Negro gamblers, trollops and truckmen, because they seemed more alive than the "professional" and precious Bohemians who intermingled with the real theatre workers, anarchists, radicals, and serious artists whom he did respect.

The hardships he endured through the years of adventure seriously undermined his health. He lived for months on the free lunches provided with drinks. He slept in airless bunks or with his head on a table. There were times when his puzzled father—for whom, being now very much a puzzled parent himself, he can feel sympathy—gave him a dollar a day. "More than I should do in the same circumstances." Not long before his break-down he was forced unwillingly to take a small part in *Monte Cristo,* then being presented in vaudeville, and enjoyed both the vaudeville actors and western cities. But the trip could not save his health, and after a few months' "cub reporting" on the New London *Telegraph,* he found himself in a Connecticut sanatorium that must closely have resembled the one described in *The Straw.*

Murray, the tuberculous hero of the play, the reporter who achieves through illness the power to become a creative writer, is one of the half-dozen self-portraits that O'Neill has sketched in his stage-directions. The play suggests also that here O'Neill met for the first time some delicate sentimental experience that deepened his faith in himself. His recent biographer, Barrett Clark, tells

92

us that Latimer, the editor of the *Telegraph,* had not only believed in O'Neill but proclaimed to his father that the boy would be famous, if he lived. Perhaps that also was a "straw" which showed the direction of the wind. In any case, O'Neill began, in a comfortless atmosphere where privacy was at a premium, to sound his own depths. O'Neill still holds a sheet of paper in a sensitive, cherishing way, as if it were precious and rare. He still writes his scenarios in a small blank book, in longhand—a round hand, almost microscopic in its self-contained exactness. The book, which will be coveted by collectors, hints at the compressed and gripping effort of will by which a sick and undisciplined man began to externalize and canalize the mass of experience which had been crowded into ten years, and laid, within the limits of a page, the foundation of a life that was at last to be his own.

O'Neill was discharged from the sanatorium after six months. He had acquired a permanent interest in healthy outdoor living and spent the next year by the sea in Connecticut, bathing all through the winter, reading voraciously in the modern and classic drama, and writing. Before he entered Professor Baker's "47 Workshop" at the instigation of his father, who was taking heart a little, he had published a volume of melodramatic one-act plays, now suppressed, called

*Thirst.* These plays, like the better ones that followed, seemed purposely to flout the intent of commercial production—and no "little theatre" groups existed when they were written. But James O'Neill had paid for their publication. And though the association with Baker was valuable and stimulating, James O'Neill had all unawares more to do with the success that finally came to the recognition of a Pulitzer Prize—fortunately before his death—than any professor. It was not for nothing that O'Neill was brought up in a stage family. His knowledge of the theatre is intuitive. Like Yank, in the stoke-hole, he "belongs." Though he scorns stage tricks and likes to condemn, for their very "trickiness," certain popular plays of his own, like *In the Zone* and *Anna Christie,* men of the theatre feel that he owes something of that "sure-fire technique," which enables him to put even symbolic drama across the footlights as a box-office success—owes also something of his grasp of pause, of climax, of the capacities of the actor's breath, to his lifelong familiarity with *Monte Cristo.*

But O'Neill also addressed himself, with his driving power of concentration and industry, to the study of Ibsen and Strindberg—who have influenced him more than any other moderns—brushed up his school German to understand Wedekind and his method. Going on to Green-

wich Village from Cambridge, he turned up in
Provincetown in 1916 with "a trunkful of plays,"
one of which, *Bound East for Cardiff*, the nascent
Provincetown group presented. This was his first
production on any stage. His first wide critical
recognition came, as is well known, from H. L.
Mencken and George Jean Nathan, who published three one-act plays in the *Smart Set*, in
1917–18. Nathan heralded him as the first great
talent in our native theatre, and was instrumental
in helping him to his first Broadway production:
*Beyond the Horizon*. Since then, with the Provincetown and later the Greenwich Theatre, where
he became himself a producer, in partnership with
Jones and Macgowan, as his "home town" and
laboratory, and Broadway as the seal of his wider
successes, Eugene O'Neill has come into a position
of undisputed leadership in the American theatre
—a position reinforced by the translation of his
works into many foreign languages and their production in European countries and even in the
Orient.

In this long list of plays, which show O'Neill
growing steadily in depth, range, and inventive-
ness, one can discern three periods. The first tends
to be romantic and objective: to it belong those
fine one-act plays first published as *The Moon of
the Caribbees*—the title play, especially, as Nathan
has pointed out, has in it the "glow" of male

youth—and, of course, *The Emperor Jones*, remembered for a fluid beauty of movement which one has missed in later and longer works. The second period tends to be naturalistic and autobiographical; it includes works as diverse as *Anna Christie*, *Diff'rent*, *Beyond the Horizon*, *Gold*, *Welded*. In the last period naturalism gives way to symbolism and subjective material is cast in a deeper, more poetic and philosophic form: *The Fountain*, *Desire Under the Elms*, *The Great God Brown*, *Marco Millions*, *Lazarus Laughs*.

The periodic division should not be overstressed because the author's habit of separate preliminary work on plays and of rewriting from a first revision, as in *The Fountain*, makes it unreal in point of time: plays of different periods often mature simultaneously. Moreover, though O'Neill says frankly now that he has "finished with the naturalistic theatre," it is in a sense true that he has never in realism sought anything but a symbol; never in a concrete hero failed to shadow Man, the eternal protagonist, in the grip of natural forces greater than himself. O'Neill, fortunately for his popularity, swims in the forces of his time as he swims in the sea. His thought is intuitively moulded by them.

*The Hairy Ape*, for example, was so truly a tract of the times that its blunt, stringent truths pinched like a tight shoe. Yet in point of form the play is on the road to symbolism—remember the masks, the sombre and startling confrontation of Yank and the gorilla in the Zoo. O'Neill admits that it was "unconscious autobiography." He chose to write about the hairy stoker, victim of modern industry, a man far removed from himself in actual circumstance, in order to voice through Yank that social rebellion and sense of buffeted frustration which was his philosophic message at the time. "I ain't on oith and I ain't in heaven, get me" says Yank, thrown out into the street by the I. W. W.s—"I'm in the middle tryin' to separate 'em, takin' all the woist punches from bot' of 'em."

Similarly, the two Negro plays, which seem naturally to grow out of an acute American problem with which O'Neill had had personal contact, stirs depths that lie beneath the relations of the black man and the white. O'Neill's recording of the Negro inflated by power and deflated by mortal fear gives a shadowy image of all human regression. In *All God's Chillun Got Wings* there pierces through the beauty and tragedy of a mixed marriage a suggestion of the deeper and more sacrificial aspects of marriage itself: a hint of the torture and the bliss that the interweaving of two strands of intense and separate life may bring. Here, more effectively than in *Welded*, O'Neill the solitary artist expresses the constant restless struggle between the separateness of his human soul and its need for fusion and immolation.

By the time he wrote *Welded* O'Neill had seen for man, his hero, the light of some desperate dawn. The dawn shows him crawling out of the bitter dilemma that had held him in the circle of his fatalism, like a creature in a trap. Is it woman who is pointing the way? So long as her presence in the plays is merely casual, so long as she is used as a trick for the pivoting of masculine fate, she is provocative of disaster, and O'Neill is more cruel than tender in his understanding of her. But when, as in *The Straw*, in *Anna Christie*, in *The First Man*, in *Welded*, in *All God's Chillun*, in *Desire Under the Elms*, in *Brown*, man has to leave his egotistic confines to meet her need of perceptive love, of children, of separateness from himself—when the family, with its bondage, conflict, tenderness, really takes the stage—then the thumb-screws of fate begin to relax their hold. Then man, by his identification with something beyond and outside himself, begins to be released. A prostitute, generic giver, may release him as well as a wife.

When played realistically *Welded* failed. Its verisimilitude was over-logical, photographic. It seems that O'Neill cannot mirror life too exactly: he needs a refracting lens—such a lens as we see in the portrait of Dion, a man who comes close to being the youthful O'Neill:

> Following them [his parents] as if he were a stranger, walking alone, is their son, Dion. He is about the same height as young Brown, but lean and wiry, without repose, continually in restless nervous movement. His face is masked. The mask is a fixed forcing of his own face—dark, spiritual, poetic, passionately supersensitive, helplessly unprotected in its childlike, religious faith in life—into the expression of a mocking, reckless, defiant, gaily scoffing, and sensual young Pan.

This mask-antique symbol which O'Neill is restoring to the stage signifies to him, it is easy to see, more than a stage trick. More even than a screen interposed between the crucial self and the bleary popular eye. It is an integral part of his character as an artist. For, as he once said in a letter to the papers, the world is not only blind to Dion, the man beneath the mask; it also condemns the mask of Pan. O'Neill has known and feared the world's sneer in the past. O'Neill the hard adventurer, who loved alcohol and found beauty in the life of a prostitute, has felt himself as much condemned as O'Neill the dreamy poet. He responded for long by giving back to the world in his plays a lurid and caustic picture of itself. A picture whose distortions—like those of the Chamber of Horrors—are never those of illusion; whose dreams

·are nightmares. But gradually, through a deep-
ening of his own life currents, which brought
reality more nearly into his grasp, the warfare between himself and life grew sterile. All his slings
and arrows had not altered the duality of the
world. All the slings and arrows of the world had
not altered the duality of O'Neill.

It was at this point—when O'Neill the artist
became clearly able to hold the screen, not only
between himself and the world, but between himself and himself—between the hard and the soft,
the weak and the strong, the destructive and the
creative parts of his own nature—that *The Great
God Brown* was born. In *Beyond the Horizon* the
two brothers have a doomed separation. In *Brown*,
they have a kind of rhythmic fusion, in which
resurrection is glimpsed. As one listens to the
funeral oration pronounced by Cybel, the prostitute, over the body of Brown—"spring bearing
the intolerable chalice of life again"—the words
seem unnecessary and over-accented. He who has
not already drawn that sense of death and resurrection from the lives of the protagonists, from
the movement of the play, has got nothing. We
knew before she told us that it was Man who lay
dead. We knew that, masked or unmasked, he
wore the face of Eugene O'Neill. O'Neill might
well forget his old trick—which fitted well with
the crosses and the desert road—of driving in his

points like so many sharp nails. He might well let that poetry he kept so long locked in his heart seep out through the movement of the play itself, rather than in consciously poetic imagery—seep out as it does in speech of Dion about the death of his mother, at the end of the first act. For style, for naked compassion and understanding, this is the peak of O'Neill's writing. Here the world of dreams and the world of reality are one.

I remember a sweet strange girl, with affectionate bewildered eyes, as if God had locked her in a dark closet without any explanations. I was the sole doll our ogre, her husband, allowed her and she played mother and child with me for many years in that house until at last through two tears I watched her die with the shy pride of one who has lengthened her dress and put up her hair. And I felt like a forsaken toy and cried to be buried with her, because her hands alone had caressed without clawing. She lived long and aged greatly in the two days before they closed her coffin. The last time I looked, her purity had forgotten me, she was stainless and imperishable, and I knew my sobs were ugly and meaningless to her virginity——

O'Neill's spiritual development and his art are so closely connected that it may happen that plays to him of crucial meaning will not be the ones "the public wants." *Welded* did not carry across the footlights as well as a complex sadistic thesis like *Desire*, which pays off many old psychological scores before the lovers are redeemed by their suffering. *The Fountain*, where man's pursuit of

illusion is treated in a minor and musical key, is
less effective than plays where illusion is exploded
with dynamite. What will be the fate of *Lazarus
Laughed,* which with its great choruses and its
quasi-Greek form suggests one of the vast pan-
oramic stages of the theatre of to-morrow, but
even more demands the actors of to-morrow?
Whether it fails or succeeds on the boards, it is of
first importance to O'Neill. For here the mask enables the artist not only to separate but to salvage
the dual nature of man. Here at last the vise-like
balance between yea and nay is broken, and the
positive element in O'Neill's nature flows forward
in a note of triumphant faith. Not the doubts of
Caligula but the laughter of the man who descended into the shadow rings out. And one sees
at last, reflected on the page, the look of happy
serenity that transforms the face of the swimmer
as he strikes out into that blue sustaining sea.

O'Neill, who, as it happens, was born on Broadway, is almost unknown there, and New York sees
but little of him. He prefers to make his home at
an old life-saving station at the end of a sandy
track over the moors on Cape Cod, or in a house
that was once an inn on the Bermuda shore.
Though he is fastidious in his daily dress—too
much so for a super-tramp?—he does not put on
evening clothes to dine wisely with the great. He
has seen only three of his own plays in perform-

ance and does not take his honours easily. He still
feels loyal to his friends the under dogs. His peers
have to come three-quarters of the way to meet
him. When he received an honorary degree at
Yale, an ordeal that he had desperately dreaded
in advance, his wife was amused to discover that
he became so interested in the spectacle that he did
finally enjoy his own part in it, and instead of
dying of stage-fright "took a bow" on the ap-
plause. But Pauline Lord tells how, on the first-
night of *Anna Christie*—his first "big success"—
he escaped from the joyous party assembled after
the play in his apartment and balanced himself on
the edge of the bath-tub—suffering perhaps, as
he always does, from the wide gap between the
performance and the idea, the need of recognition
and the fear of it.

It would take more than the hypothetical
O'Neill Repertory Theatre, more than a Michael
Arlen success, to make him other than a solitary
artist, struggling to work out new form, new content, in the drama. His tendency to telescope long
time periods—as in *Desire* and *Brown*—is increasing. Soon we shall see a play that will have the
length, breadth, and thickness of a novel. His
self-confidence, inside his shell of shyness, is absolute. The range of his imagination knows no
limits. He gives the impression of being still at the
very beginning of a career which is incalculable,

except that it will be precipitate, fertile, concentrated, and solitary.

When O'Neill steps lightly along some pagan shore with Shane, he walks a little behind, a tall figure, in a bathing-suit, with limbs burnt to a pagan blackness: and on his face the look, not of a "father," but of some trusting elder child who has grown up into a strange world.

# CHAPTER VI
# ELINOR WYLIE
*Intricate and Crystal*

ELINOR WYLIE

*Camera Portrait by E. O. Hoppé*

## ELINOR WYLIE

*Intricate and Crystal*

HIS high-spirited girl, who moves, for my mind's eye, in the stiff brocaded folds of an Infanta, was, as the old English saying goes, born with a silver spoon in her mouth, in a world that Henry James, Edith Wharton, and Amy Lowell could understand and picture. At one-and-twenty, having been married still earlier, she threw the spoon on the floor and decided to be an Enchanting Companion. To speak truth, she and her sister and brother, her real intimates, in her Washington childhood, had always questioned the feel of cold silver in their mouths, and teased their brains with poetry. So off went Elinor to live in England, in the New Forest, with the fawns and the deer—another Jennifer Lorn intrigued by another Honourable and haughty and cultivated Gerald Poynard. But the deer of the forest are haughty creatures too, though they seem so innocent. There is a look in the bland, touching eyes of fawns, especially, that drives a creature hysterical with longings that are not fed by sheltering beech-leaves, lamp-lit evenings of love, and ancient books.

So, in due course, the witch returned to her native land.

> Now why should I, who walk alone,
> Who am ironical and proud,
> Turn when a woman casts a stone
> At a beggar in a shroud?

The Maine coast, which she had always loved, was her favourite haven. There, being after all unhappy, rather lonely and unoccupied, wandering one day about the house, she saw the gleam of a slender silver object in the corner of a deserted room. It was a PEN. She recognized it because she had tried it first in her early youth, picked it up in the New Forest, and thrown it down in a quick despair—one of those fits of wilful self-distrust which the men who have loved her have made it their business to soothe and beguile. She liked its slim, elongated shape, exclaimed with horror over its tarnished surface, and polished it tenderly to the metallic sheen that she exacts of all the objects that surround her.

So, in a humble room, wainscoted in yellow pine and over a grocery store, Elinor Wylie ceased to be an Enchanting Companion and began to write poetry, a lonely art. The beat of the northern winter sea was in her ears. Little lost islands, cedar-grown and wave-washed, swam before her eyes. "She began, very softly, to sing the lament for Flodden; her extreme happiness made her voice more than ever mournful and forlorn." Poor Jenny Forlorn, we shall not be too sorry for her, since she was at last finding her real self. The poetry, like the pen, had a gem-like gleam, recalling Amy Lowell's. It had a cadence and a form and a content reminiscent of another lonely woman, who, by dint of asking God unanswerable questions, produced great epigrammatic poetry in an Amherst garden. Some of Elinor Wylie's question must have been answered, for, as she sat there, lost and writing, the pretty curves returned to her discontented lips and the gleam of merry malice to her childish eyes, which are, by the way, hazel in their colour.

In due course, again—for I must abridge this semi-symbolic tale—she left Washington "for good," yes, surely for good: conventional society was not her real home. She took a room in University Place, like any other struggling young writer who wonders where she will get the money to pay her landlord. But she arranged there—to the amazement of the clever young gentlemen who forthwith came clamouring to take her out to dinner—a series of fashionable drawing-room chairs, straight out of Edith Wharton and Henry James again, most resistant to lounging literary backs, though so exactly suited to her own straight, unyielding elegance; and in addition embellished her surroundings with certain luxurious and grandiose objects that amazed the Bohemian eye. There was a "flower-piece," that, though bought in a junk-shop on Madison Avenue, might have graced her mother's drawing-room in its most official days. There was a pale blue and white lamp of English Wedgwood pattern, no doubt the gift of an ironic sentimentalist, which had travelled with her far and wide, and which she cherished like a baby. There was also a very elaborate silver mirror of the same period, swung on a silver standard (for she is a "Prinkin' Leddie," and rubs rouge on her palms as she talks). There were old books in choice bindings. And the young woman whom you saw in the midst of this crystal disharmony still wore the same silver dresses, with the same worldly elegance. But there was a difference. For Elinor Wylie for the first time in her life was free.

"Her influence over the prince's mind was a constant source of wonder to the girl, who had invariably played the part of feathered shuttle-cock to the obstinacy of others. Her husband had always appeared completely unmoved and imperturbable; she marvelled incessantly to behold her curious power in regard to the temperamental Abbas——" After all, you see, she was not continuously, could not be, a Lonely Poet. The Enchanting Companion tracked her down; the Young Lady of Fashion reappeared, with her tastes and requisitions, and even her pruderies; the Collector of *objets d'art et de luxe* confronted her like a ghost. Ancient selves (not so very ancient), ancient conventionalities, were her Lares and Penates, and she was writing for *Vanity Fair* under a frivolous name. Courage she had never lacked, and while she was finishing her first and most exuberant novel, and, as usual, keeping her bureau drawers and her fine frocks in perfect order, she was marrying for the third time—taking to herself a faithful and affectionate literary husband, who belonged, rather oddly, to the world of her dead brother, and yet lived in the very centre of literary New York.

Discovering the world of fiction, as distinguished from the world of society, the world of romantic and cynical adventure, the world of hard payments, the world of lonely poetry, Elinor Benét, once Wylie, *née* Hoyt, hurled herself headlong into it, and became still another Elinor, whom I think of as a Lady in a Dream. If you observe her tossing off a cocktail in the small hours with the Algonquins, you will think her

III

perhaps just the latest celebrity. Her popularity is
a toy that she thoroughly enjoys playing with, for
she has, has always had, as *The Venetian Glass
Nephew* tells us plainly, the gift of play. She has
put aside her conventions as unsuited to her en-
vironment, for she has "never liked to hurt people's feelings"—as she would say. But she leans on
a simple and selfless devotion, and really lives only
when she is shut up for the day in an empty room
with her Lares, to which have been added a few
eighteenth-century bird prints, a solid Benét comfort or two, a typewriter, and a can of Campbell's
soup. She may still indulge herself in a great state
of pique, but she never lets it—indeed never did,
since she sees herself so clearly—interfere with
her heavenly flight with her dear Shelley across
the United States of 1822. Now there, if you ask
me, in this ideal figment, this figure of the Orphan
Angel, is the man she really loves, as Amy Lowell
loved Keats. Have you noticed how careful Elinor
Wylie is to protect him from the other ladies,
those who live not as she, in a dream, but desir-
ously? Not once, between the Atlantic and the
Pacific, is this lover of women permitted to receive or to give so much as a kiss. Even Anne,
the debonair white daughter of the red Indian
chief, who might be another Elinor, is permitted
only to touch the tips of his moccasins with her
lips.

Better to see your cheek grown sallow
And your hair grown grey, so soon, so soon,
Than to forget to hallo, hallo,
After the milk-white hounds of the moon.

Charming poetry, and sincere, but not to be
taken literally. Elinor Wylie can look, on occasion,
a harrowed woman who has known tragedy. She
can be tender to the under dogs and chivalrous
to the unsuccessful, like that lost brother of her
youth who felt life too deeply to bear its tragedy
as she does, with a smile and a touch of rouge.
Her cheek is never anything but rosy, and I can
imagine the storms that would arise below Fourteenth Street if a single white hair were espied in
those tawny locks which are always bobbed and
waved as for the ball of a debutante. How often
and how exquisitely has she described herself:

But you have a proud face
Which the world cannot harm,
You have turned pain to a grace
And the scorn to a charm.

You have taken the arrows and stings
Which prick and bruise
And fashioned them into wings
For the heels of your shoes.

What has it done, this world,
With hard finger-tips,
But sweetly chiselled and curled
Your inscrutable lips.

ELINOR WYLIE walks with the firm, elastic tread of one who knows she has a blooded charger in the stable of her mind (he is shod in silver) to ride afield at will. Sometimes the animal chafes at the bit, tosses foam to the stars. But once astride him, she is master of him, and mastering, their blood runs fast and furious, as they together leap insurmountable obstacles with an extraordinary skill and virtuosity. The woman is, as the French say, still young, and has produced, in a very short time, and under pressures none too easy to adjust, two volumes of poetry which placed her at once among the most sensitive, poignant, and accomplished of the American poets of the day, and three novels—poet's novels, all three, especially the last, *The Orphan Angel*—expert in their craftsmanship and mature and delicious in their own extravagant and artificial vein. Elinor Wylie has always been conspicuous; that is her nature; but the most conspicuous act of her life was to emerge, as a finished artist, with no period of fumbling or apparent preparation. Like Athena, she seems to have sprung in her "black armour" from the head of a god.

Was it life's enrichments, or life's deprivations, that tempted the pleasure-loving, the spoiled, the delicate, the brittle, the elusive Infanta, insolent and elfin as a child, to live alone with a typewriter in an empty room?

Down to the Puritan marrow of my bones
There's something in this richness that I hate.
I love the look, austere, immaculate,
Of landscapes drawn in pearly monotones.
There's something in my very blood that owns
Bare hills, cold silver on a sky of slate,
A thread of water, churned to milky spate,
Streaming through slanted pastures fenced with stones.

That "Puritan marrow" is real; I am reminded again of those Puritans of an older day, Henry James, Amy Lowell, with whom she belongs in spirit, if not in generation, who forced a cultivated power into the strait, strict field of art. How different the cool dove-coloured, icicle-pointed battles of her mind from the realistic earthly struggles of a Dreiser; from the tense emotional wrestlings of a Eugene O'Neill! Yet the Puritan brain is no easy antagonist:

My body is weary to death of my mischievous brain

And again:

It is my thoughts that colour
My soul that slips between;
Thoughts lunar and solar
And gold and sea-green

Tint the pure translucence
Of the crystal thread;
A rainbow nuisance
It runs through my head.

Could anything be more exquisitely devised than a Venetian Glass Nephew fabricated by Casanova to release a quicksilver soul from lunar and solar thoughts?

> From shackles frailer
> Than the wind-spun sea.

Yet here is a poem that seems to sum up, with Yankee vigour and an eighteenth-century clarity that reminds one of Zélide, the ultimate Elinor Wylie, marrowed by the Puritans and twisted by the cynics:

> Now let no charitable hope
> Confuse my mind with images
> Of eagle and of antelope:
> I am in nature none of these.
>
> I was, being human, born alone;
> I am, being woman, hard beset;
> I live by squeezing from a stone
> The little nourishment I get.
>
> In masks outrageous and austere
> The years go by in single file;
> But none has merited my fear,
> And none has quite escaped my smile.

That last line suggest a favourite quotation of Elinor Wylie's—it was said of Thomas Love Peacock—"He likes the flavour of an imperfect world and the preposterousness of peccant humanity." No wonder her books are delightful to Max Beerbohm. The urbane, ironic tone of Jennifer Lorn, which does not demand that the world be perfect but only that it be diverting to the cool and laughing mind; the conceit of the Venetian Glass Nephew, these are similar to his own tone and conceit. Yet behind the mind in Elinor Wylie I catch a glimpse of

> . . . a weeping creature
> In a glass-walled cave.

In *The Venetian Glass Nephew* the sound of weeping is more audible to me than in *Jennifer,* and I am not surprised that the porcelain lady breaks her china bonds, and with a cry of very human high spirits dashes off across the continent, tenderly companioning a poet whom she has adored since childhood. There is more of warmth in *The Orphan Angel* than in the earlier books, but it is still the warmth of a cold stream in the sparkle of noon. Perhaps it is because I have stood on the selfsame mountain height that I love this passage about the traversing of the Sangre de Cristos: "Shiloh was like a blue-eyed eagle as he stared into the sun. Some transformation of glory was performed within his own mind, so that its

actual convolutions came to hold the meaning of
the crystal universe and to exalt it into a clear,
abstract perfection of language; there are those
who would sell their souls into darkness for a
knowledge of the syllables which flowed like a
stream of snow-water through Shiloh's mind."

> The bird Imagination
> That flies so far, that dies so soon

—he is Elinor Wylie's darling. He perches, like a
bright-winged parakeet, on her slender wrist.

Yet I remember the poem called "Beware!" in
which "Baba, Playing a Nocturne by Chopin," is
enjoined not to drown in sorrow:

> Baba flourishes and dips,
> Little gestures poise and gleam;
> Now her shiny finger-tips
> Strike the surface of the stream.

> Now she plunges both her wrists
> In the water blue as air,
> Curdling into starry mists,
> Diapered with light despair.

> Deep above the drowning sands
> Sorrow like a moon is drowned;
> Baba, only dip your hands
> In the surface of the sound.

Will the Lady in a Dream, who is the novelist of airy reconstructions, break one day the shiny mirror which she holds between herself and the world and, as she promised in another poem, called "Valentine," in her most perfect first volume, eat her own honey-sweet heart? Elinor Wylie's dreamface is strange in its cold, silvery detachment when seen across a room, yet so childishly hard-hearted and friendly, when she talks of her gambols with curling lips, who can say what it promises, what it withholds? All artists have a right to their limitations, for their limitations shape their art.

THE true story, O high-spirited Infanta and Porcelain Companion, would nevertheless be worth telling in fiction. What is the source of the crystal fountain that throws its sparkles to the sky in the park of Versailles? In what dark soil grow the roots of the tree of white flowers into which you were once nearly transformed in a conservatory to avoid the ardent embraces of a human young man, my charming Jennifer? Where did it really travel,

> This soul, this vanity, blown hither and thither,
> By trivial breath, over the whole world's length,

O harrowed woman with the hollow breast and the sarcastic sigil on your brow?—you seem to tell so much, and yet how little, how little, you really reveal!

These remarks and queries, and others equally inquisitive and outrageous, I may have had in my mind when I climbed, the other day, the stairs of that highly respectable apartment house that you are promptly deserting in a childish rage or an ancient despair, or a reasoned sally, because the fire-escape annoys you, obscures with its ugly, utilitarian shape the polished glass window where, poised over the world's abyss—deep-gouged Grand Canyon into which you dare not look for fear of giddiness—you write down your dream on the twinkling keys, one perfect word after another, with never an erasure or a doubt.

But you seemed absent, and contemplated your bright-pink thumb-nails, with your near-sighted stare. The gaudy parakeet you cherish was hopping about your table. Surrounded by the heaps and heaps of books from the Public Library in which you conduct your cryptic researches, you remarked inconsequently that, being a witch (I always knew it), you could not give me the Metropolitan Tower, but that there was a very little locket, made out of a wild-cat's skin, which might tell me something if I carried it in a dark pocket.

"What would Mamma say, what would my dear Jane Austen say, if I really wrote it all down?" you murmured, with a troubled air, offering a rosy cheek to the peck of the insistent bird, playing with the silver pen which, as I did not fail to notice, lay, gleaming like a charm, beside the typewriter.

"But that is exactly what Jane did," I murmured back, not too tactfully.

You turned to me in a cold but polite impatience:

"Don't you see that you are spoiling my dream with this senseless interruption? Don't you hear my horse outside the door, champing his silver hooves? I should think anyone would know that he wants to be off for Salem——"

With a squawk of inchoate sympathy the tropical bird clapped his rainbow wings over your proud, unruffled head. So, like the Forsaken Merman, a creature from a northern clime, contritely and sadly, I stole out:

> Children dear, was it yesterday
> (Call yet once) that she went away?
>
> Singing: "There dwells a loved one,
> But cruel is she!
> She left lonely for ever
> The kings of the sea."

## CHAPTER VII

# CHARLES TOWNSEND
# COPELAND

*Copey of Harvard*

CHARLES TOWNSEND·COPELAND

Camera Portrait by E. O. Hoppé

# CHARLES TOWNSEND COPELAND

*Copey of Harvard*

HARLES TOWNSEND COPELAND is one of the few legends that Harvard University has produced. A thin, caustic, discreet little man, with a large head, a meagre if carefully erect body, and rather pinched and greying New England features, he does not look at first sight a legendary figure. You might pass him in the Yard in an east wind, steering an armful of shabby books, and think you had noted a "professor." But "Copey" does not mean "professor" to Harvard graduates and undergraduates. His appointment last year to the Boylston chair of Rhetoric was not a tribute to academic achievement in the usual sense. It was the tardy recognition of a unique influence.

The influence has centred in Hollis 15, whose square-paned windows, high among the branches of the elms in the north end of the Yard, have been a night beacon to many solitary or sociable young souls, and many sentimental *revenants* from the larger world beyond the gates. In this mellow academic domicile, a relic of the Harvard of the eighteenth century, at the head of three naked and worn flights of steep stairs, the Copeland who receives his guests begins to manifest his spell, and define his characteristics.

He comes obviously from the state of Maine, for one thing—any good New Englander will recognize the winter apple flavour, the accent, clear and crisp, the species: one of those "old" families who esteem themselves highly—highly and acutely. I should expect a man from coastal Maine to pick out such a room as this, for crabbed tenantry and courteous hospitality of thirty-odd years. The three flights of stairs give a kind of advantage of height as well as a kind of seclusion. The early American flavour is reminiscent. There is safe comfort within—fire-light, candlelight, oil lamps, panelling, and walls of books, yet the windows are fit for scanning distant seas. The host announces that his great-grandmother Townsend read Pope's *Odyssey* to her daughters and servitors as they made the Thanksgiving pies. A proud, sturdy race, appreciative, as it has had to strive for them, of the good and honorific things of this world.

The room is comfortably populated and full

of quiet talk. Responsive young men, much at home and at ease, fill the background. The honoured lady—"I can make one Queen o' the May—I don't know how to administer two or three, having the fate of Paris in mind"—sits on the left of the glowing hearth. On the right, the host —a conscious celebrity, you would say, maintaining with whimsical crusty speech an attitude. A "character" who likes to usurp our pleased attention. A slightly pompous Johnsonian character, with Lamb-like quips, and Carlylesque locutions, declaring, when pressed, literary judgments discerning, direct, kindly, and modern beyond the mannerisms. And all the while, the man behind the "character," the man himself, leaning back in the morris chair, with the single gas-light beside it shining on the forehead rising to his bald head, a trim, oldish figure, in a grey suit, with stiff Puritan back and air of perfect correctness, requires and expects a deeper definition. The grey face, with its eager eyes and vivid sudden smile, is almost poignantly sensitive and sharp with some inner light of feeling.

The young men seem aware of it. Do they realize that this Harvard personage has given practically the whole of his life to the entertainment, the illumination and admonishment of students like themselves? That they are not to him merely themselves, as they sit in their chairs, but symbols of the generations that pass like the leaves of the elms? The evening at home may be changed from Monday to Wednesday—so a notice on the door proclaims—but the institution is immortal, and to how many such generations has Copeland read, as he will read to-night!

Will he really read? Yes, but first there must be fussy consideration of lamps and windows. This should be up, that down. Now the spectacles are lost. They must be in the office, two flights down. Off shoots the scout, called back for the key. The *right* key, Charles, have you the *right* key?—here. The young men busy themselves with tolerant and affectionate solicitude.

At last things are approximately and impermanently right. Copeland, with the fully focused attention of his audience, opens his book.

> Thou wast not born for death, immortal Bird!
> No hungry generations tread thee down;
> The voice I hear this passing night was heard
> In ancient days by emperor and clown.

The voice, the passing night!—it is Copeland's true voice that speaks at last. The voice has sharp Down East inflections, its range is limited, but its sympathetic magic is potent. It leads one, by an art rarely histrionic and profound, through the dreaming vistas of Keats's poem to the heart of the Copeland legend.

The centre of every man's existence is a dream, they say—Chesterton says it in his essay on Scott. Deeper than habits, calamities, and sins lies his vision of himself, "as swaggering and sentimental as a penny novelette." Copeland's dream is no more sentimental than any other man's. But because it is an histrionic dream, its swagger is more visible. The manner, at once indifferent and vain, the superficial weaknesses, as crystalline as those of a child, and of much the same sort—the sort that need and claim approval and affection—seem to shield the dream of an artist of the stage. A highly accomplished and sophisticated artist, fertile in the discovery of means to enforce his power. An artist who never speaks from the stage without seeing himself from the audience. Yet also an intuitive artist, who, like any fine actor, makes to his performance the supreme gift of himself.

A college campus is a stage, a platform is a stage, an academic chamber is a stage, if you choose to take it so. Here a man indisposed by temper or tradition for the actor's rôle may come into his own. I am not suggesting that when Copeland entered the Harvard English Department, as a humble corrector of themes in another man's course, he had any such conscious aim. He may not even have suspected that he had something personal and pre-eminently human to give the university that would more than compensate for lack of formal scholarship or higher degrees. But it is a fact that he did not strive to remedy his academic defects. He did not drudge for a Ph.D. —the Boylston professor still lacks that mark of academic prestige. No, from the beginning his time and his heart went into his own peculiar educational inventions. That quasi-tutorial relation with his pupils, and with innumerable boys who were not his pupils, those voluntary classes in "reading aloud" which the Harvard men of the nineties remember with such warmth, though they did not contribute toward a degree, those public readings for "Town and Gown" in Sever 11, began almost immediately, and almost immediately made a name, and created an audience.

Copeland recalls how instinctively, at his first reading, in that intimidating Sever amphitheatre, he turned his chair from the sober elder townsfolk —from the past—to face the future: college youth. That, of his many audiences, was not only the first but the real and final one. Youth could understand, as age could not so surely, the inspiration welling ever fresh out of the histrionic dream.

Most professors of literature present neatly dissected masterpieces to the minds of their students. Copeland has done very little dissecting. He has poured masterpieces whole into the souls of his hearers, with a peculiar fervour of speech and accent that seem, though so perfectly in control, the discharge of some inner compulsion. What we see, especially inside a book, we may ignore. What we hear, really hear, in that fashion, we *feel,* like a kind of music. Literature and life fuse, or, rather, literature becomes the flower and consummation of life. The great writers of the past, the figures of their creation, are living, actual, understandable, ourselves. At their best, Copeland's reading of prose and poetry and his biographical lectures have had a breath of living genius.

That indented Maine coast where he grew up, among blue inlets, rocky isles, and tidal rivers, has, for the dreaming mind, the aspect of "faëry lands forlorn." The old Maine stock, from which he comes, is leisurely and beauty-loving as well as pioneering. Aristocrats of the provinces, as good as anybody and even a little better, they are ever scornful of mediocre performance in life. The ghostly inward whip which they lay upon the shoulders of their descendants scourged Copeland, I feel sure, to prove his mettle in the world, to leap obstacles, by persistent courageous effort. And he certainly owes them the slighting accents with which names not loved, like Byron's, are dismissed from his lips; the caustic touch which seems to throw the light of some inward scorn upon his own peccadillos. These Maine folk are not very easily fooled, even about themselves.

It was on January 1st, 1825, that Charles

Townsend Copeland's grandfather Lowell, descended from the second son of Percival, arrived
with his wife in Robinston, twelve miles beyond
Calais. His grandfather Copeland, on the other
hand, was born in Boston, and migrated only as a
young man to Norridgewock, on the Kennebec,
where he edited, printed, and published a very
creditable newspaper. The Boylston professor,
born in Calais in 1860, comes of four long-lived
lines. He was the first of the lot to go to college,
and to that fact he chooses to ascribe his lack of
application to formal learning.

Graduating from Harvard in the class of 1882,
he began in the uncertain manner of the artist
race—to which we must admit this unprofessorly
professor belongs—a series of attempts to adjust
to the practical world. The most important were
seven years of dramatic and book reviewing on
a Boston newspaper. Here Copeland began to
affirm the major passions of his life—interest in
human beings, and books and plays and great
persons, especially great persons of the stage, like
his old friend, Minnie Maddern Fiske, and those
others, Bernhardt, Modjeska, Booth, Jefferson,
whose photographs hang on the walls of Hollis
15. In the year 1892, at two-and-thirty, on his
own application, he became an instructor in the
Harvard English Department—then ruled by a
group of pundits of Germanic scholarly tradition.

In his official rôle he remained an overworked freshman hack until the year 1905, when Dean Briggs asked him to renounce freshman teaching and take on an "advanced" course in writing. This, which proved an outstanding contribution to academic Harvard, was his first original teaching opportunity. He began also, with the honourable, if anomalous, title of "Lecturer," to give those favourite literary courses of his—Lives, Times, and Characters of Men of Letters, Johnson and His Circle—humane courses both, stressing great men and great character, which brought the past to life by a process of recreation rather than erudition. Though Copey seemed addicted to the young man's world, he was never one of those Harvard professors who scorned teaching women. He taught at Radcliffe thirty years, in fact, and has no more loyal adherents among Harvard than among Radcliffe graduates, who recall with gratitude the standards of literary taste he inculcated, the fresh interest he stirred in dead classics, the unobtrusive, even tender kindness, the frank abusive, derisive criticism, which young women were advised to take "like men." In University Extension work and Summer School teaching, he had similarly a marked popular success.

The Harvard Corporation made Copeland an Associate Professor in 1910, eighteen years after his first appointment. His Boylston Professorship,

in which he succeeded Dean Briggs, came again
fifteen years later, at the age of sixty-five—the
age which in many colleges is that of retirement.
Probably no other university in the country would
have given a teacher so much freedom and so little
recognition.

This slow gathering of public laurels had, however, its own advantages for Copeland. A *rara
avis* among professors, a brilliant and somewhat
"misunderstood" figure, who signified to his students, in a way they could scarcely define, the creative spirit, he engaged ardent loyalties and pro-
voked curiosities usually denied to figure-heads.
What other professor has an alumni association of
his own?—The Charles T. Copeland Association
brings "Copey" on to the Harvard Club of New
York every winter for a much "featured" occasion, a dinner and a reading which draw former
students from all over the country. Would Copeland's Christmas mail arrive in a truck, would
those postcards from the faithful be forever in
circulation, and those Harvard war letters fill
several treasured volumes if he had not been for
the greater part of his career a Pretender rather
than a Prince? For that matter, would Copeland
have become "Copey," the teacher who "took the
curse off books"; would he have developed so
surely into the tutor-at-large, the avuncular guide
and philosopher, whom Harvard and Radcliffe

youth was proud to call friend, if there had not been in him that X-quality that does not fit into professorial pigeon-holes?

Young American writers like to say, resenting the fact that they were over-taught by the meticulous, that writing cannot be taught at all. Copeland has no more over-taught writing than he has over-dissected the classics. His war upon dullness and bluff has been inspired by first-hand knowledge. He knew, from his personal experience in the newspaper world, something very definite about writing as a trade, and did not confuse journalism with literature. Like most teachers who take their profession with passion, he soon abandoned his secret desire to write, translated it into terms of other men's performance, past and future.

Certain little "editions" of the poets, with prefaces, appeared in the early Harvard days, an edition of Carlyle's *Letters to His Sister,* and an excellent short *Life of Edwin Booth,* which reveals much of the author's love for the stage. But writing is an exclusive business and Copey, like the mother of a family, did not have the heart to close his door.

"Who is it?"

"I'm James Smith, and I'm drunk, drunk, drunk!"

"Come in, drunken James!"

The door of Hollis 15 was not always on the latch, but it opened readily. The men who came, stayed. Their troubles, financial and amatory, their ambitions, their dreams—perceived almost before they were spoken by that sensitive perception, that power of vicarious identification with others which is Copey's, not only because he is himself, but because he has the literary and dramatic temper—became his own. Like a soul in migration he left his body to enter their wide future adventures. This youth must be urged to go round the Horn, that one sent to Oxford, this one assisted to a newspaper job, that one provided with a sound, remunerative business opening, or a wife with money. Meanwhile all must be urged to read, and "badgered" into doing good work. It is easy to see how they became charges upon a heart at once tender and humane, and a judgment worldly-wise. Gradually they aroused an interest so exclusive that it crowded out all personal ambition save that sole aim of influencing youth to read and write, and to comport itself well in the world.

The words of his former students are the surest commentary on his original method of teaching in English 12. The crux of it is a three-quarter-of-an-hour interview, every fortnight, in the Hollis office, in which the student *reads his work aloud* to the listening teacher. The method of the ear again—it was originated by chance, at a moment

when Copeland could not use his eyes, and had to
correct papers orally. But he quickly discovered
that he had fallen upon a real pedagogic discovery.

On the occasion of my first conference [writes a recent
student] he sat staring, out of an open window as I read. In
the beginning I felt as though I were reading to emptiness
outside the window, that none of my "gems" were being
heard. I soon discovered that I was woefully mistaken. My
"gems" were being considered, most of them condemned. I
was told that they were bad, and why they were. I was made
to see that the first approach to writing lay in humility, the
second in honest sweating, not the arrogant confidence possessed by most undergraduate would-be *littérateurs*. At the
same time I began to see where the honester, unconsidered
portions of the theme were better, and again why. All this in
little comments which I had to jot down in the margin.

At the end of the conference I took from Copey's dictation his final opinion; and from that I learned the following
things. First, that he was as sympathetic with all my efforts
as I was myself, that he understood what I was trying to do
and how the doing of it hurt. Second, that he was as humble
in criticism as he made me feel I ought to be in learning to
write, that he was living the helper to my individual needs
and giving me a great deal of himself in doing so—that he
was not dictating his opinions, and respected my views, if I
was able to offer any proof of their validity.

He was always alive to the change and thirst for change
in undergraduate character, and where he did not agree was
able to sympathize. I began to realize his amazing freshness
of mind and his understanding of undergraduate ambitions.
In what would appear to be his narrowing confinement in
the Yard, he has drunk so long of the spirit of youth, and so
deep, that it has enlarged his soul. Copey will never be old.

Copey rules the class room as he does his public audiences with a kingly sceptre that has a malicious reach for the heels of rebels. This gifted and singular personality, imprisoned in a thin and constricted frame, this teacher whom his most perceptive pupils have seen from two angles, the real presence, the stage presence, cannot tolerate an audience that is not wholly *his,* even to its coughs and sneezes. (That solemn admonition, *"Don't* cough—*don't!"* is oddly effective, even in the season of *grippe.*) Rows over steam-pipes and windows, to the abashment of terrorized janitors; demands for glasses of water that are not drunk; quips and cranks and savage gibes: these are most charitably interpreted as methods of concentrating attention.

It is reported that he arrived late one day in a Harvard class, with a melodramatic air deliberately overcharged.

"Gentlemen, gentlemen, I have just had a fearful adventure. I was crossing Harvard Square, holding a book that my friend John Reed has just sent me—a volume inscribed to his old teacher—and one of those *devil-wagons* [taxis] nearly ran me down. I thank God, gentlemen, that I had it in me to hurl the volume at the head of the driver. It fell into the back seat. It went on to Boston."

The books from former pupils would make a sizable library and be sure that Copey is as ready to read from Robert Benchley or Heywood Broun as from Kipling or the Book of Ruth. Men like John Reed, far as the poles from Copeland in political and social horizon, never become less close: "Is it just *inside* the Kremlin or just *outside* the Kremlin that Jack is buried?"

Copey's Reminiscences—one of those famous books that will never be written—("Come for the manuscript in eight years," he wired the last applicant) would make a very complete inner history of the Harvard of the last thirty-five years. The golden period, so far as Copeland's own life goes, would be the twentieth-century years that preceded the war. During the war he made himself an informal recruiting-sergeant, as did so many men in the fifties, deprived of action themselves, and got out of the letters of his young friends a fine vicarious satisfaction. Since the War the objective new generation, under the sway of heroes of their own invention—the sceptical Strachey, the hard-hitting Mencken—query a little all that savours of "appreciation" as well as of mannerism in Copeland's biographical method. Yet there he still sits in Hollis 15, no longer technically a hero who needs support but an elderly gentleman with a well-organized tradition,—visited frequently by Barrymores and Bishops,—and, at last, an academic crown.

But the men who work with him—instead of

visiting him like a museum specimen or a Harvard "sight," feel that Copey is unchanged. "Copey can never grow old." Nothing, if the truth were told, neither the academic honours nor the Charles T. Copeland Association, can alter the angle from which he looks, is condemned to look, at life: for it is the remove of the artist.

Copeland speaks in his *Life of Booth* of a man's debt to his career. His own debt to Harvard is the opportunity the university has offered for the satisfaction of a profound love and sympathy for youth. He speaks also, in this book, of "the separate pang" of the actor's lot, who sees the spiritual body of his art crumble before his natural body. That is, in a sense, for all his rich rewards, the prospective pang of this teacher whose sway owes so much to the histrionic dream. For Copey must, though surrounded and protected by ardent youth as few elders are, live ever solitary and by proxy, at the top of his creaking stairs. He must, to the end, yield up his personal essence as a sacrifice to his masters and let them speak their mysteries through his lips.

A highly sophisticated auditor attended one of Copeland's readings at the Summer School a few years ago. It was such an intolerably hot and stale July evening as only the Cambridge midsummer can provide. Copeland began with one of his best Biblical selections. But there was little response from the benches, and he felt it. Suddenly rising, he gave a keen glance about the hall. Then, quietly, he turned out the lamp beside his chair.

A signal that the reading was over? No, something more symbolic. It was, rather, as if he had turned out the personality of Charles T. Copeland. In so doing, he summoned the personality of Lady Macbeth to rise out of the dimness.

He did not read. He did not recite. He did not act, in any definable way. By an *intention* only he achieved the tragic presence of that eternal sleepwalker. But it was enough. The spectator went out from a hall, now tense and magnetic, with the sense of having had one of the great dramatic revelations of her life. Something to set beside a performance by Booth himself.

# CHAPTER VIII

# PAULINE LORD

*One Stung by the Gadfly*

PAULINE LORD

*Camera Portrait by E. O. Hoppé*

VIII

# PAULINE LORD

One Stung by the Gadfly

 AULINE LORD has the power to create images of feminine desolation that linger for years in the memory. The wavering, visual image which, in *They Knew What They Wanted,* seemed to symbolize Amy's adaptation to the maze of trouble in which she found herself is still fresh and moving. But who can forget the image of fear—stark, quailing, nauseating fear—that she gave in *Samson and Delilah,* when she grovelled along the wall, to escape the erotic vengeance of Ben Ami? Or the image of tenderness, suppressed and hungry girlish tenderness for a father, triumphing over a pitiful distrust of men in general, that she revealed in the first act of *Anna Christie,* with nothing more tangible than an arrested phrase in a stale and husky voice, and a flutter of speaking hands?

The impression of her Anna Christie was so

145

final that one can scarcely conceive an Anna built
on the strapping, Viking-daughter lines of
O'Neill's stage-directions. And this is not because
of Anna's flat, Minnesota drawl, or any other
superficial verisimilitude: it is because of Pauline
Lord's accurate and poignant betrayal of emotion.
Betrayal, rather than portrayal. This actress reveals emotion unwillingly, as sensitive women do,
and with a minimum of instinctive physical
movement. Instead of holding up her feelings to
the public gaze, she raises a kind of translucent
screen between them and the audience. It is by accident that our eyes pierce her reserve; by necessity that our hearts quiver at the sharpness of the
sword on which her life seems to turn.

The creature knows authentically that interior
*frisson* that lies at the heart of drama. Such secret
moments of illumination as she gives deepen the
whole art of acting—make it in reality a noble art,
with a long echo in the human spirit instead of a
tricky performance where complacent or striking personality, or shrewd intelligence make their
effects. This actress, too, has intelligence; but it is
the sort that crystallizes unconsciously in the
blood. She has personality; but it is as subtle and
fugitive as an innocent remembered scent of
childhood. She has, finally, a fascinating little face,
mobile and sensitive; but only a modernist, drawing from memory again, rather than from obser-

vation, could evoke it by some fleeing line which would symbolize the moods—wilful, unreliable, excessive, tortured, vindictive, persecuted, pathetic, terrible—at the back of the dramatic temper. Out of the moods, rather than out of any fixed corporeal shape or beauty of her own, emerges, in its wholeness, the character and presence she is representing.

Off the stage Pauline Lord can look—yes, even now, at the height of her powers—an *ingénue*. The hands and feet, which she uses so sparingly yet so evocatively on the stage, are small, the waist is tiny, the frame slight and yielding. Her brown eyes have a startled look in the pale oval of her face. Her straight little nose, her sensitive, curved red mouth, her mop of tawny hair, which always straggles a little and is done in an old-fashioned pompadour, would fit a Barrie heroine. Yet even in adolescence—she has been acting since she was thirteen—she was not chosen for *ingénue* parts. Her directors recognized in her gift something sterner. Nat Goodwin gave her at seventeen such maturities as the rôle of a poor insane old woman in an asylum, mistreated by her keepers.

THE Hotel Plaza is a conventional place to have tea with a prima donna. There I went, to find a slight, shy figure, dressed up in dark-blue, hiding under a big hat, and with no airs of celebrity.

147

Pauline Lord actually wanted to escape attention. Talking vaguely and politely, with fidgety little feminine gestures, she might have drifted in from some middle-western town. She was not quite at ease or at home. Her dark eyes flickered. Her voice hesitated, trembled into huskiness. And then came a light nervous laugh—it came, like a cuckoo trill from a clock, with a hint of mysterious "works" one had not penetrated. A laugh is after all the thing that reveals the hidden vibration—be it roguishness, unction, asperity, fear—that dominates every human spirit.

That pensive, oblique sound gave me a vision of the woman. Pauline Lord herself. Of course she sat opposite to me, nibbling a cake. But also she was not there. Very much not there. I had a glimpse of her looking at me from behind a gilded pillar; appraising me; wondering: "Is this one of the people who will charge dentist's bills against me? Impersonate me? Sue me? Do me dirt?"

I tried to lure her back to her deserted seat by talk of the theatre. But my language was intellectual: she looked at me blankly, as if I spoke in riddles. "Praise to the face is an open disgrace," in New England. My word of admiration was awkward enough. But that was not why the actress retreated further. The only shrewdness I see in her is a seasoned doubt of the face value of

words and persons—like Anna's first doubt of her
father, like Amy's doubt of Tony's good intentions. But this delicately sceptical person would, I
perceived, discount the Greeks and their gifts for
another and finer reason: there is in her some
inviolable severity, some deep humbleness and
sincerity that is beyond compliment and even
beyond praise. Though she were surrounded by
panderers and flatterers they would not really
touch her. She would only lend them the fume
and froth of her more negligible personality.

"I never talk about the theatre—not crazy
about it as a profession—so little help—nobody in
my family really interested in the stage—never
even keep my notices——

"I can't act—*really* act—unless I am unhappy
or nervous—true happiness somewhere else—I
have to say to myself: 'Pauline, you must earn
your living'—sometimes I wonder why I can't be
just normal—those people are much to be envied
—a little commonplace happiness——"

The voice whispered like a ghost.

Another time—it was driving in the park on a
hot summer night—she murmured: "I can't bob
my hair." Nor was the remark inconsequent.
Pauline Lord's whole silhouette is long-haired, persecuted, escaping. The best Paris dressmaker could

not make of it the hard, chic, declaratory outline which every little stenographer picks up on Broadway; as the best Paris coiffeur could not discipline those fine ravelled locks that escape from under her hat and, in a dramatic crisis, are pressed back convulsively from stricken temples. I began to define this wistful woman who sat staring into the night, her head bent like a flower too heavy for its stalk, by a series of further negations. Nobody can "dress" her, set her off, not even that resourceful Robert Edmond Jones, who has done it often for the stage. She cannot capitalize her glamour, in the manner of the second-rate heroine, or—this comment she supplied herself—command attention by "carrying on" like a prima donna. She tried hysterics once. She thought she had reached the point where she could afford to—but they didn't work. And to tell the truth she can't see an actress banging her head on the floor without thinking—"Do you suppose it is those years of hard work?"—that it is "funny."

"There are so many things to be sorry for in the world," went on the veiled voice. "I wanted to get some birds for my porch—songsters—I sent to a dealer—he said he had only one left—it wasn't worth selling—it wouldn't sing, it was ugly—well," breathed tenderness, "I wish you could hear that bird now, singing in my rose-bushes——"

ONCE she nerved herself to talk a little of her method of working. This is an approximation: "Off stage anybody can do anything to me—I don't know how to get what I want. I am uncertain.

"But on the stage I am different. I know exactly what I am about. I am sure. Oh, not at first. I have to study hard, so hard, to struggle, get to rock bottom—I think I am going to fail (I always think that—I need help). But finally I see—every word, every action, every intonation, every movement, is clear to me—and I hear myself saying, right out, to people—oh, I give them their rights and their due, but I keep my own—I say: 'Don't you *dare* to stand there, do this, speak that way——' "

ALL converse with Pauline Lord must be impressionistic, fragmentary. It is as if you never in the everyday world saw her save in a half-light, never heard more than a half-word. But in twilight the pupil of the eye becomes dilated and intent. So out of these vanishing vignettes, these indefinite phrases, and out of the transcendental comment of those who have worked with her on the stage, one gets a spectral image of how she lives and functions as an artist.

First of all she is an intensely subjective actress.

Her sources of power are inspirational, intuitive, almost mediumistic. The clue to her artistic destiny leads in a direction diametrically opposed to that of an actress of the Russian school. Take a Knipper-Tchekhova: her solid and redundant humanity seems based on a kind of group consciousness that reinforces her subjective contribution. The Moscow group, seen at a private party, give almost as unified a sense of background and tradition as a group of church-goers in an old-style New England village. Not so a group of Broadway actresses. Put Pauline Lord with her emotional receptivity beside Clare Eames, with her nervous intelligence, Katherine Cornell, with her earthy fire, Eva Le Gallienne, with her self-enchanted egotism: one sees, not a group, but a series of brilliant individuals, shooting each at a personal tangent. The companions of Pauline Lord are not her sister actresses, but her twin selves, the defenceless mortal, avid of happiness, and the sure artist driven to a consummation that spurns happiness, held by a sort of duress in one skin.

If she belongs, as I believe she does, to a great dramatic lineage, it is by virtue of this doubleness of being, this peculiar temperamental endowment, which enables her by a kind of abnegation to invite into her wistful, human self a second self—an alien female, like Sidney Howard's Amy. She cherishes this non-self strongly and profoundly, as a mother a child. The girl fits inside her, takes the rhythm of her blood; and when she finally reveals her, in her nakedness, it is as flesh of her flesh. Whether you call Pauline Lord "great, great, great," in the words of Heywood Broun, or put her lower in the dramatic scale, you cannot ignore her temperament, which in kind is like that of a Duse or a Bernhardt. You may call the gift it fosters integrity of imagination, you may call it "inspiration," if you like. You may give it, as Jones and Hopkins do, a more mystical explanation.

"Why should an actress be a 'person'?" (Jones was staring with visionary detachment at the receding banks of the Hudson.) "Characterization on the stage is a kind of divine incarnation. The 'character' is at once the guest and the adversary of the body it occupies. Consider the strain, the terror, for the tragic actress, of being at once the host and enemy to this divine phenomenon— the only one of our time."

Arthur Hopkins, the director, who first among managers discerned Pauline Lord's true powers, speaks almost religiously of her access to the eternal verities. This chubby little brown man with his round brown eyes that gaze inwards, his nubbly red apple cheeks, thinks of the theatre as of a church where the artist talks to God. Sitting in his office, he said of Pauline Lord—always gazing inwards—something like this:

"Artists cannot be dissected—Pauline Lord doesn't know where or how or when she gets what she does. But if there is such a thing as Absolute Truth, that is what she achieves.

"I believe we all have in us a register of all the emotions. Leonardo da Vinci was no different in essence from the rest of us. He only had more power to draw on this universal reservoir. Pauline Lord can reach it—her reading of a part has the absolute sureness of a hypnotized person, who has been commanded to do thus and so, say this or that. Everything she does or says has the beauty and exactitude of something that comes from a region of final truth. She is like Meller—the artist freed by a flight from reality, into herself."

THE story of Pauline Lord's dramatic progress is the old theatre story of the struggle, courage, disappointment, fatigue of making a woman's way alone through years of grilling hardship to that success which is called "glorious"—how the actress shakes her head!—and runs exceptionally long. What distinguishes the career from many others is its peculiarly baffled and unprotected quality. Pauline Lord was not sustained by the sense—which, after all, so often proves false—of a great artistic destiny. (Even now she does not think of herself as an "artist." She finds it disconcerting to hear the word used of herself.) She was not sustained, or projected toward achievement, as so many actresses have been, by the faith and consecrated exploitation of some second person—she travelled her path quite unaided, with the family whence she came gradually trailing in her wake; doing her utmost to be a good actress—doing it humbly and self-distrustfully, and often rebelliously or reluctantly, yet with no power to turn back from the path she had chosen. When a pretty, gentle, dependent, tender, fugitive girl with a strong pity for the under dogs of the earth shows this inflexible quality you can be pretty sure she is foredestined to go her own way. Pauline Lord was, it seems to me, a foredestined tragedienne. Life had to treat her ill. She had to be unhappy in love. The iron had to enter her soul. "Nobody knows," she repeats as Lucy Carpenter in *Sandalwood*, "nobody"—with that tremulous upward quaver which marks the meeting of endurance and self-pity—"nobody ever *will* know what I've been through."

She is a Californian—born in the San Joaquin valley, educated in a convent in Woodland. It was there, in the convent, in a school play, that she had her first success. Though she was only a Negro maid, she became the most important person. Yet she cannot tell you just why she went on the stage. There were no dramatic traditions in her family, except that her father ran away as a boy and went into vaudeville for a while. She only knows that when her people moved to San Francisco, she used her allowance of twenty-five cents a week to go every Saturday to a matinée, walking back and forth, a long distance, because there was nothing left for carfare. And at thirteen, she was studying and beginning to act in the school of the Alcazar Theatre, run by Belasco, the brother of the New York producer. John Craig saw her there, playing in a small part when she was fifteen, and said that she was like Mrs. Fiske. "That meant nothing in my life. I had never heard of Mrs. Fiske. I had never heard of anybody. If he had said that I was like the leading lady of the theatre, I should have known what he was talking about." Nat Goodwin also saw her, called out to her from the wings that phrase—often quoted in accounts of Pauline Lord—which lighted her ambition: "Burn a little oil, young lady!" He saw that she was gifted and casually told her to look him up when she came to New York.

There was nothing casual about the girl's response. Pauline took him literally. After the San Francisco earthquake, she gathered her savings together and came on. She was sixteen then. Nat Goodwin was more surprised than delighted when she walked in. He engaged her for a run on the road. But after all, she was neither fish nor fowl and he sent her home from New Orleans. Heartbreaking—somehow, she got back to New York again. But she had no luck and was glad enough to find an opening in a stock company in Milwaukee.

The next years were stern. It seemed that this girl was not made for good fortune. Her first New York appearance was under the management of Harris, in *The Talker*, by Marian Fairfax. *The Talker* was a hit. But then came seven or eight plays that were doomed as soon as they came on. She has no special patience in reciting the chronicle. What is the use?—ancient history.

The important thing is this: she was, through all these years, struggling with dramatic technique. At first she strove—being superficially adaptable and indeed conventional—not a revolutionary in any sense—to live up to the instruction of her various directors and managers. "Stand here, move there. Say this, this way [like some popular actress probably]. You're underplaying. What do you want playing melodrama as if it was Ibsen?" Somehow or other she could not please them or adopt their tricks. Somehow or other she was building up confidence in her inner convictions. But she took her directors like the rain.

"What shall I do?" she asked Arthur Hopkins, mechanically, when she began to rehearse *The Deluge,* her first play under his capable management.

"Do anything you want."

"Can I *really* do anything I want?" Shaken, she walked in, went over to the table——

This first moment of creative independence was her emancipation and her victory. Pauline Lord regards Arthur Hopkins with gratitude, as her only dramatic teacher. He says he taught her nothing. Nobody could teach her anything. He could only, he says, give her confidence in herself: confidence to make her contact with that inner guide which, through travail, leads her at last to truth.

From *The Deluge* she went to *On Trial, A Night's Lodging, Samson and Delilah,* where she had her first long run as star. *Anna Christie* followed. The play ran for two years in New York, then in Chicago and on the road, then in London, in 1922. Here the actress had the great triumph of her career. She was panicky beforehand. Jones relates how her tears flowed into her plate when he took her out to lunch. She was sure the traditional English coldness was going to drown her in a frigid tide. After the first performance the audience stood up and yelled. The play was called the greatest success of the London stage in twenty years.

"After Duse and Pauline Lord, who is there?" asked Clive Bell. She was recognized by the gallery that stood hours in the rain, by the critics so much more severe than our own, as an artist of the first order, who had gifts beyond the range of any contemporary English actress.

These gifts, in *They Knew What They Wanted*, were the instrument that discovered to the public another new talent in the young American theatre. The play had a strong popular appeal and ran for more than a year in New York and then on the road. In the rôle of Amy, the California girl from the "spaghetti joint" who engages herself by correspondence to an Italian wine-grower and discovers too late that he is old, Pauline Lord had a character emotionally naïve and pathetic, occasionally tense and high-pitched, whom she could endow with the truth of her temperamental faculties. O'Neill declares that *Anna Christie* has tricky and theatrical spots, and the same is true of *They Knew What They Wanted*. Neither offers an actress a great rôle in the classic sense. Pauline Lord played Anna and Amy as if they were classics and gave them a final realism. Any playwright with a core of sincerity is safe in her hands. Even in a confused piece like *Sandalwood*, where she plays the dull and tenacious wife, she achieves clarity, pierces through dross and dullness to the inalienable truth of marriage, and makes visible its inexorable law. And we know precisely why. As the critics of an older day would have said: "This is what it is to be an actress. This is what it means to 'walk the boards.'"

WHERE, on our stage, which loves stereotypes almost as much as our factories do—on our stage so rich, so wasteful of great talents, so accidental —will Pauline Lord end? Will she ever be allowed to develop, through use, the full range of her powers—which include those of a remarkable comedienne—as a continental artist of her calibre would surely do, in some honourable and endowed repertory company? For answer, I hear only the echo, pensive and oblique, of the actress's laugh. Pauline Lord, though the high-brows have now discovered her, has been ground in the mill of the American commercial theatre. It has both scarred and tempered her, taught her to bend without breaking, and crowned her with its own jewels. Besides, it is not for nothing that she reverences O'Neill's understanding of human suffering. Not for nothing that she loves to salvage tiny yellow canaries to hop briskly about her rose trees. Not for nothing that she flutters herself, so lightly, so sadly, about the cruel snares of life.

Ask her why she came to be sought to represent the erring, the unfortunate, the traduced of femininity, and you will get no very clear answer, beyond a sigh. But one thing is clear: as a feminine being, Pauline Lord is elusive, wistful, quivering, tormented. As a woman, she is defenseless—the doe pursued by the huntsman. She is harried; Io stung by the gad-fly. It is only when she is before an audience that this torture becomes a fulfilment and an ecstasy. On the stage, the pursued quality of the woman takes on the aspect of Fate, Nemesis. The hunted quarry becomes the Tragic Victim.

## CHAPTER IX

# WILLIAM ALLEN WHITE

*Merry Gentleman of Emporia*

WILLIAM ALLEN WHITE

*Camera Portrait by Loomis*

# WILLIAM ALLEN WHITE

*Merry Gentleman of Emporia*

 HE editor of the Emporia *Gazette* is as picturesque and salient an American as ever came out of the corn belt. He has a salty tongue that twists platitudes into Platonisms or epigrams which the plain American can relish. He has light-lashed blue eyes where "the fair, fond visions of youth" still linger, though he is on the road to sixty. He has a solid and fleshly form, and a double chin, and instinctively wears his hat on the back of his head or slouched over his nose. His strong, broad mouth stretches naturally into a quip or a beaming smile of welcome.

That beam, from the warmth of a heart that is like the sun in its beneficence, means something. If I were in trouble, I should send William Allen White a call for help. If I wanted to make a French financial expert understand the figment called "American idealism" which young Ameri-

cans themselves have discarded, I should en-
deavour to have the cynic borne on a magic carpet
over the Atlantic, over New York, over Chicago,
over the cornfields of Kansas, and deposited on
the hospitable front door-step of a certain red
brick house in Emporia, which, to my fancy—
perhaps because I have several times broken a
western journey there—stands in the very middle
of our broad continent. White speaks somewhere
of "charity, which lends humour her eyes." Charity in this sense is the law of his life. The "Ameri-
cana" he collects, and for which he has as great a
zest as Mencken, are coloured with it. His ob-
servations of men, events, and manners, even the
most acute and broadest of them, have no sting.
He enjoys and respects intelligence, but he suffers
fools tolerantly, and enters into all human hearts
with something of neighbourliness and of reverence.

I met him at the last Democratic convention in
Madison Square Garden. Expanding, exuberant,
shrewd, perspiring, unvested, he looked the figure of a mid-western politician. The day was
piping, the presidential balloting was indecisive.
But as he grasped my hand, the mental weather
changed. The world, which had been whirling in a
hot cloud of popular destruction, spun again in
a clearer ether. Perhaps there was something in the
party system of government, perhaps there was

something in Democracy. Bill White, you see, is a Believer, though politics do not fool him. He is far too perspicacious for that. What interests him in politicians, as in men in general, he would tell you, is not their mechanical or chemical or material compound but their hidden virtue. "The thing that makes toward *good*." He is not afraid to use the antiquated word. The dynamic drive that creates conflict, and enables agitators like Bryan to open the road for the Roosevelts and the Wilsons is of passionate concern to him. He sees the Roosevelts and the Wilsons with a certain detachment, but he likes to think, as Mencken does not, that they are great men with faults, or at least faulty men with streaks of greatness.

W HITE is identified for me with a vision of the American genius that came to me when, journeying early in 1918 through the American "Line of Communications" in France—the place where the inconspicuous, hard-working non-militarists were standing deep in mud, improvising storehouses and airplane factories and roads and railroads and docks with neither materials nor tools, I lunched with one plain and undistinguished countryman after another, dressed up rather scrubbily as an officer. The lunch was likely to be poor, straight out of an army can. There was never, as at an officer's table in the French army, a neatly written menu, resting against a mellow winebottle, there were no young peas and delicious omelet for whose ingredients an attentive orderly had foraged near-by farms. In fact there was no outward evidence that things were, in spite of war, "for the best, in the best of all possible worlds." Yet one knew that the officer, lonely and delving, was thinking things good, and therefore, like a pioneer, *making them good.* There was something here that a woman, travelling also alone, could put her faith in, say: "This is what an American is, adequate, courageous, resourceful in emergency, unassuming, protective to women, and full of a secret tenderness."

White, of course, had no pioneer job during the war, in spite of *The Martial Adventures of Henry and Me,* but I found myself thinking of him as of the race of those officers of the rear, who could stand knee-deep in mud and never know it. He appeared in Paris as a journalist at the time of the Peace Conference, and it was clear that, though he was using to the utmost his faculty for thinking things good, he was having a sorry time of it. He had come to France, as he goes everywhere, with the mission of moralist and the zest for fearless, spontaneous action that is one of his essential traits. Roosevelt said of him: "*He preaches what he practices.*" The peacemakers were preaching very prettily. But in practice the French would not let him meet the Bolshevists at Prinkipo. Kansas, he once wrote, is an inferiority complex against the tricks and manners of plutocracy, social, political, economic. The tricks and manners of Paris diplomacy were quite as alien to the editor of the *Gazette*. What was it all about? Every now and then you could see, as the head tilted back, stealing into those blue eyes, round and pale, as they gazed into the distance, the dream of the Ideal President and the Disinterested Conference of World Powers. He could not bear to believe that neither existed. He was always hunting for them in the highways and by-ways. One spring Sunday I met him with an armful of bundles and the sun-warmed look that in him indicates a sentimental satisfaction. He had discovered the Rag Fair, which is largely attended by the humble citizens of Paris. These plain little bourgeois citizens, inhabitants of the many small towns that make up the great city, he could understand. There had been communication in some universal language. The Parisians of the faubourgs were real folks! And he had bought some brass candlesticks and old lace to take home to Sallie.

He lived at the Hotel Vouillemont, and entertained his friends in a dining-room full of eminent Americans, and others who were trying to be more eminent than they were. The French food was good. But sweets were scarce, and at the end of the meal, the stout and sandy host, whose rotund proportions fitted ill into his Red Cross uniform, whose chins rolled rebelliously over a stiff military collar, would send his appendage Bill, then a young gentleman of seventeen, also dressed in a Red Cross uniform, to fetch a certain tin box. It contained crumbling cookies and, as I remember, *fudge*—Sallie had sent them and Mary had made them. How dewy was his gaze, when it fell on these Kansas delicacies, how wistful and remote! How keen and warmly receptive, when it encouraged the view of the man across the table! To the top of White's honest speech rose his whimsical humour like foam. In the bottom of the glass was the wine of kindness. The atmosphere of peace was turgid enough: but here was one single-hearted man, limpid and reasonable and aspiring.

THE snowballs of liberalism that William Allen White aimed at the diplomats missed fire. But he has had a sure eye for the worthy stiff necks of his fellow Kansans. Himself wherever he goes, he is never so much so as in his state and town—in this solid central area of the United States, which knows no echo of the restless sea, no doubts of its own prosperities and securities. White has been saved from the smugness of the successful Mid-westerner who is also a Yankee Puritan, by his Irish doubts and hopes. He likes to talk of his

dual nature, as if it were a sort of Jekyll-Hyde inheritance. It may be that what conflict there was
made him a writer. He has confessed that for the
sake of his independent writing he remained a
country editor. His keen appraisals of men and
events, of national policies and personalities,
brought him, very young, openings into metropolitan newspapers and political office. But he
knew the law of his own nature and followed it by
digging into the soil where he was born and identi-
fying his needs and hopes with those of the "plain
American people." Though always earnest, he has
never been solemn about anything—except perhaps his novels. It gives him an incredible amount
of pleasure to seat himself, with his wife, outside
the *Gazette* office on a Sunday afternoon, against
the protest of the ministers, to follow the World
Series on a score-board.

Most of the honour and the power he has had as
a national influence have come from the fun he
has had in being a genuine local character. White
has for thirty years been wielding political power
without political office. The Emporia *Gazette,* or
White through the *Gazette,* has led an honest
ruling group with little or no organization, and
enforced his representation in city, state, and national politics by men who believed his way. Yet
the *Gazette* is a local sheet with 6,500 subscribers.
White's suggestion that he would like an invitation

to Sunday dinner is not seen more than fifty miles from the office. The editorials are widely read only because they are copied by the press of the whole country.

When the editor met me on a certain August afternoon, on the platform of the Santa Fé Railroad at Emporia—a division point where the western trains pause for breath—with the thermometer at 104, I thought I understood the secret of his authority. His whole person, his thick, tough body, his shrewd, ruddy realistic face, where tiny lines of tenderness have formed about the eyes and mouth, gave out a sort of radiation. As the cornfields exude fertility and the shrill cicada's chant rises above the heavy heat, so does a kind of genial excess quality—an earthy vitality and pungency—exude from the editor of the *Gazette*.

The newspaper has been the mirror of his personality, and both the paper and White himself are one with their Kansas town in a way that an Easterner will scarcely understand—unless he reads the paper, or that selection of its editorials, which is White's best and least-known work. A flat little prairie town, nourished in the lap of endless cornfields, with two colleges in its centre —yet White loves it as if he had made it, and you might say he had done just that. At the sight of the modern high school tears almost rise to his

eyes. The place was largely settled by New Englanders and it has that prim and self-respecting
look, though the elms lack the proud individual
spread of the New England centenarians, and the
streets are too straight and uniform, and the hills
and Colonial outlines have been forgotten. But
not the Puritan aspirations! There are institutions
of learning and progress to every square inch.

But the soul of Emporia, the institution that
makes it unlike other prairie college towns of fifteen thousand modestly prosperous, industrious
inhabitants, is a shabby little newspaper office.
Driving in the Dodge, with Mrs. White at the
wheel, and W. A. W. enriching the road with his
humane, vernacular comment—explaining, for
instance, how the solid Republican Walrus he used
to be turned into the Progressive March Hare—
we arrived at the holy of holies. He showed me the
presses, old and new. He showed me, with a twinkle of mischief, Bill in his shirt-sleeves, using his
Harvard polish to coax new subscriptions to the
*Gazette* out of the hard palms of farmers' wives.
He explained his method of profit-sharing, and
his shrewd method of serving the community and
the advertisers at the same time. And then he took
me home—to the house that is, like himself, all
gentle-hearted abundance.

> The world is so full of a number of things,
> I'm sure we should all be as happy as kings.

White's favourite illusion that he is a typical, small-town Kansan breaks down a little in his home. He likes to tell a story of how his father and his uncle, whose own father had come from Massachusetts with the pioneers, bought plug hats and store clothes and went back to visit their Boston relatives—and met with such a "frost" that they quickly returned to the democratic warmth of Kansas. The paternal plug hat, symbol of snobbery and inferiority, stayed on a closet shelf, and White can scarcely bear to have Bill wear one, even in New York. He himself takes pride in being, in dress, manner, and custom, a native son. But no Madeiran loves his copper wine-jug, no Arab sheik his flaming embroidered hanging, more than this pluperfect Kansas family their loot of exotic foreign lands.

"Bill got home last month," says a letter, "he brought a tremendous lot of European junk—it pleased his mother." Caruso lives eternally in Emporia, not by a song, preserved in metal, but by a succulent *risotto* made from his recipe by the hand of the Kentucky hostess. Mrs. White, as my grandmother would have said, sets a good table. The association is direct, for devotees of gastronomy like the Whites are few in the United States since the old New Englanders and old Southerners passed away. The smiling host in the rocker on the garden porch, surrounded by books and newspapers—I seem to remember that he had removed his coat—appeared, after a few sample meals, richly to deserve his curves. Prohibitionist though he be—an editor whose "tipple" is "frivolling"—he is no pale ascetic, but a man of passion and solid appetite.

W HITE is the first to admit, with a genial gleam of self-observation, that there is nobody he likes better to talk about than his favourite hero. His autobiography should be his masterpiece. It will evoke, as do the flashes of reminiscence and the bits of Kansas history that occur in his daily writings, the vigour and the sweep, the rainbow hope, and the bitter hardship that have now all but faded out of the prairie country. He can look farther back than most Americans of sixty, for he was the only child of a middle-aged marriage, and his paternal grandfather was born during the Revolutionary War. From Raynham, Massachusetts, this adventurous forbear journeyed in a prairie schooner to Ohio in 1801. His son moved on to Kansas in 1859. He was a pioneer doctor and merchant, a picturesque character, and married in his late forties an Irish emigrant from New York state who had driven into Emporia on a stagecoach while it was still a pioneer settlement, a hundred miles from the railroad. William Allen was therefore a true child of the prairie, born in

Emporia, brought up in El Dorado—the very names, which strike the superior traveller on the Santa Fé as funny, are to a native monuments of the poignant illusion and the courage of the pathfinders.

"When I was a year old, Emporia became too effete for my parents and they moved to El Dorado, Kansas. There I grew up. El Dorado was a town of a dozen houses, located on the banks of the Walnut, a sluggish but a clear and beautiful prairie stream, rock bottom and spring fed. I went to the large, stone schoolhouse that 'reared its awful form' on the hill above the town, before there were any two-storey buildings in the place."

This boy in his free hours roamed the prairie in a gang that shared the wonders of the unspoiled natural world—hunting, trapping, fishing, "the last shadow of some ancient and innocent hour left over from the Eden of the race." But he was never allowed to forget the schoolhouse and all it implied. His mother was "the sort of woman who walked on her heels and is known as captain," and the major passion of her life was education. Left an orphan at the age of sixteen, she managed, after her westward move, to acquire a good education in a small Illinois college. When in middle life she had a child of her own, and had, against her will, to bring him up in a tough town where "the dark and greedy life" of the plains was manifest, where gamblers and prostitutes camped in the big timber and drinking and shooting were the life of the community: she read to her boy to keep him beside her—read to him before he was twelve *Middlemarch* and *Adam Bede,* most of Dickens, and even George Sand.

"My mother had always wanted two things—a watch and an operation. My father had his pride. He said she had a good clock and was never out of the house, so what did she need of a watch, and, being a doctor, he knew perfectly well that she did not need an operation. So these desires were repressed. When I was fourteen he fell sick and died, largely of a broken heart." (He was a Democrat and his candidate was defeated.) "He died Thursday. We had the funeral Saturday. He was mayor of El Dorado and the funeral was in every way satisfactory to the Irish heart of my mother. Monday she took me by the hand and went down town and bought the best lady's watch in El Dorado. In a few weeks she was planning for an operation. But when I cried and begged her not to leave me an orphan, she sighed and gave it up."

It was perhaps now that White acquired the "swelled head" which he declares he has "spent his whole life trying to keep up with." He had to go out and collect his father's rents. He was fourteen, and he shouldered responsibility lightly. "I have just naturally taken it ever since." A postscript to this sentence is his wife's: "He can't be an hour on an ocean liner without telling the captain how to run the ship." Like his wit, his robust and contagious laugh, and even his fatness, leadership seems a congenital and lovable gift.

He himself claims luck as heritage from his Irish grandmother, Anne Kelley. When things went hard in northern New York, the girl cleared the floor, lifted up her skirts, and began to dance and sing. That gay-hearted grandmother has always opened the way for him to jump. (When I asked him what luck was, if muscle or a mystical self-confidence had nothing to do with it, he shook his head at me: "High-brow stuff! Try that below Fourteenth Street!")

During his first year of college in Emporia he discovered that his mother had opened a boarding-house to keep him. Three letters were despatched to El Dorado; to the dry-goods merchant, to the grocer, and to the printer, asking for a job. The printer offered one. Luck! When White returned to college with an afternoon job as printer on the paper that is now the *Gazette*, he roomed with the reporter, a superior youth who was also "college orator." Soon the reporter departed to an oratorical contest, leaving his job in trust to Will; forgot his speech: never dared return to Emporia. So —bull luck again!—White became a journalist. At the age of twenty-four he was already editorial writer on the best Kansas daily newspaper.

In those years he was a rock-ribbed Republican and the Kansas City *Star* was Democratic. So, though his "head-size" increased in Kansas City—I am quoting authority—he found the politics and the dominion of his elders very irksome. Having married, as one would expect, a school-teacher, that charming Miss Sallie Lindsay, white-skinned, black-eyed, black-haired, who has never lost her Kentucky accent or the observant humour that moulds her lips, he decided to look about for a newspaper of his own. It must be in a college town, the two young people decided—that was the place to bring up children. The Emporia *Gazette* was in the market. White bought it for $3,000 without a cent in cash, "with the audacity and impudence of youth." Then, with his very male strength and energy and ability, he proceeded to make a success of it.

He started in, boldly and simply, as "Parson Pierrot" to his fellow Kansans, "guide, philosopher and friend, executioner and undertaker, promoter and herald, preacher, teacher, autocrat and judge." Beside him—literally beside him in the office—was a girl who could practise domestic arts and carry her share of a venture without claiming to be more than a wife. In the background was another "feminine influence," the dominant Irish mother, who continued to live next door to her son till she died at ninety-five. In the foreground, nursed in the office waste-paper-basket—a big clothes-basket—was young Bill, growing up to love the smell of printer's ink. Mr. White attended to the business end of the paper and wrote the editorials. Mrs. White did reporting, social news—everything else. In three years the mortgage was paid, the first volume of stories was published, and White had made by his editorial, "What is the Matter with Kansas," a national name as a political writer.

Remember that White was a conservative and a vehement young fighter. He had grown up in disorder, and acquired his privileges with a degree of effort that made the worship of privilege natural. So meeting some Kansas Populists in the post office, being one against many, being licked in argument, having a sick wife in Colorado and a lot of copy to write before he could join her, he "executed" the Populists. To him, the piece seemed no different from any other editorial. But it was seized upon by Mark Hanna as a campaign document and reprinted in every Republican newspaper in the country. White was already known as a staunch party Republican and Hanna sent for him and inquired what office he would like as political reward. The editor of the *Gazette* answered sturdily that he had bought his freedom dear, and wanted only to keep it.

The answer reveals that basic consistency of character that has given White the trust of the plain citizen. Consistency of opinion he has never claimed. His writing has been the fruit, ripe or unripe, of the hour. "All the public has a right to ask of the editorial writer is an honest mind, a kindly heart ribbed with courage, such intelligence as the day's work may bring." Behind White the writer is a propagandist, whose writings are action—rugged, moralistic. He has asked little more of the world than the chance to act in this way; to carry out, through untrammelled, uninhibited speech, an honest and fearless purpose which, like his personality, has something of the unction of the preacher.

THE history of White's political career in Kansas, and its national connections will no doubt be written *in extenso*. One of its historic dates was the meeting with the Populists. Another and greater was the meeting with Theodore Roosevelt —greater because it brought about that shift from right to left in opinion which was the most sensational event of the editor's spiritual maturity.

White and Roosevelt first met in 1897, and took to one another like brothers. White was already damning McKinley and Hanna under his breath for their crass material philosophy, and craving a new political direction. When, in 1900,

Platt named Roosevelt for the vice-presidency
to put him out of the presidential running, White
saw the forces of privilege which he had wor-
shipped in a new and lurid light. "We held lodges
of anger and wrath together." After Roosevelt's
sudden elevation to the presidency, White found
himself happily on the side of nonconformity. He
had no qualms or doubts at the shift. He knows
no such thing as remorse or introspection. Like
Roosevelt himself, he moved to the left because he
could not move otherwise. Such men take the
shape of their times as water follows the contour
of the earth. The altruistic-progressive trend in
politics exactly fitted the idealist-reformer in
White. His faith in the leaders had declined, but
his faith in the people was growing, and Roosevelt
seemed to represent them.

Since then every crisis in the social evolution of
Kansas, every national—and lately, international
—struggle for liberty and justice, has found the
citizen from Emporia ready to leap the barricades
and engage in active fighting. It was foredestined
that he should give Labour its due in the rail strike
of 1922—proclaiming "49%" sympathy with the
strikers, in a poster forbidden by his friend Gov-
ernor Henry Allen, but displayed just the same
in the window of the *Gazette* office; increasing it
by 1% a day while they refrained from violence;
getting arrested, winning his point of law; writ-

ing one of his finest editorials about it, called "Lines to an Anxious Friend," that won the Pulitzer Prize. It was certain that he would call the bluff of the politicians and for the first time break his rule by running as an independent candidate in the state elections of 1924—touring three thousand miles in six weeks in the family Dodge; winning one hundred and fifty thousand votes from the elements that had no spokesman—Negroes, Catholics, Jews—just in order to define and defeat bigotry in Kansas, as embodied in the Ku Klux Klan. His gift for turning a dull piece of reform into a sensational and falstaffian adventure has made William Allen White, and the quaint doings of Emporia, journalistic "copy" of the first order in the national press, and thus given his causes weight as well as lightsomeness.

When White writes something polite before a political campaign, the other editors of the state raise a cry: "Here is the old boa constrictor again, slathering his victim with saliva before swallowing him whole!" It has been his principle to give even to the corrupt political opponent the benefit of a personal doubt. He attacks him not as a man, but as a mouthpiece or victim of ideas that are alien. When his point is surely made, he does not even rub a towel over the wound. He follows "the law of kindness, the great unwritten law of America." His estimates of our political leaders—Roosevelt, Wilson, Coolidge—astute as they are, are too kind for the melodramatic and sadistic temper of the day. White has fewer illusions than before Woodrow Wilson made his great failure, but his "epitaph" still sounds the note of hope:

> God gave him a great vision;
> The devil gave him an imperious heart.
> The proud heart is still;
> The vision lives.

While telling his readers how to eat watermelon, and what is love; while urging "sweet Alice" (the congresswoman) not to "ferment," he makes clear that "the surest fact in history is the growth of society." He rejoices to point out that solid Republicans are now Populists—"the sun do move."

White stands out as one of the significant figures in a prairie civilization that is gradually assuming the common American shape, and by that alteration losing much of its original virtue. The Emporians of the future, with all the advantages White has helped to bring, may not be men as strong and as free as himself. His combination of innocence with force and astuteness is an endearing product of the pioneer west, something which, like his dislike of a plug hat or his comments on the Walrus, a Britisher cannot well understand. Kansas is a state of personal journalism. But White will not be "placed" in journalistic history by the side of his parochial brothers. He will be reckoned the last outstanding American editor, after Watterson, who did not cloak himself in anonymity. White has had no secrets from his readers. They have shared with him, as his friends have, "the fun he has had getting rid of his theories," as they have enjoyed his personal happiness and sorrowed with his tragedy, and he has given them of his journalistic best—a best whose professional ethics can be estimated by his much-quoted estimate of Frank Munsey:

> Frank Munsey, the great publisher, is dead.
> Frank Munsey contributed to the journalism of his day the talent of a meat-packer, the morals of a money-changer, and the manners of an undertaker. He and his kind have about succeeded in transforming a once noble profession into an 8 per cent security.
> May he rest in trust!

Few Americans have as great a personal popularity as William Allen White, favourite of the "mass" magazines. His periodic visits to the National Arts Club are a holiday for a motley crew of friends. I remember the puzzled face of a visiting French professor of economics, who had accepted Sinclair Lewis as the great American novelist when he met a living man from Main Street and heard him—beaming on everybody— let off his incomparable gibes between twenty flying runs to the telephone during a single lunch. The Frenchman understood White as little as White understood the Poincaré or Berthelot crew. How could a serious Frenchman understand a humour which sees around the low-brows, sees around the high-brows, and sees W. A. W. without weakening his purpose? He can call himself in one breath "the Harold Bell Wright of ideas," "who doles out predigested intellectual food to the masses," and in the next admit that he has never consciously written a pot-boiler: that the writing he does outside his daily job, which has "provided the meal ticket for the *Gazette,* and, through the *Gazette,* for politics" is the most sacred part of his life.

All his books, except perhaps *The Court of Boyville,* his most tender extravaganza, even his novels, like *A Certain Rich Man,* are theses, formulations of the controversies of his spirit, as related to his section of the country. White lacks imagination in the higher fictional sense, he looks out rather than in, and his realism, though richly documented, is coloured by an idealism which in novels tends to come out in the accents of Parson with Pierrot omitted. "Queer things are not important," he wrote in connection with an Emporia scandal—details of divorces and murders are not, by the way, reported in the *Gazette*—"they are its kindnesses, its nobility, its self-denials, its

great renunciations." This is dangerous doctrine
for a novelist. To the greater among them, even
those idealist ladies, George Eliot and George Sand,
whom White heard read aloud as a child, queer
things have been important, along with the rest.
White knows far better than Howells, as well as
Lewis or Ruth Suckow, perhaps, what is going on
behind drawn blinds in small towns, or on dreary
farms. But—is it because he got so close, so young,
to the "dark and greedy life of the plains" and
because his mother fought to show him something
else, precisely through novels?—there are matters
he would rather tell about. Let the young people
who have had all that modern progress can do
claim the heritage of darkness. He who had to
struggle for brightness has another message. Yet
did he struggle? White is the least smug and self-
righteous of mortals. Sweetness and light are no
choice with him. They are what he may not violate.

White was born knowing the combination of
life. Chemical or mental, this equable adjustment
is his genius. I have seen him in the disguise of a
spick and span and very canny Puritan business
man, looking through his eyeglasses and down his
nose at a newspaper: obviously a church member
and a Director of the Rockefeller Foundation.
(That is the way he looks in most of his photographs. His physical contours automatically con-

geal to present the more regular of the two fellows
he harbours.) I have seen him in the disguise of a
sentimental Celtic agitator, overflowing and soft-
hearted, defender of the simple and oppressed. But
his double gifts seem made to amend and stabilize
one another. To the end he remains as whole as an
oyster, as sustaining as a staff, as jocund as a
spring zephyr.

The jocundity and the fecundity which always
come out in life and in editorials give him something of the flavour of an Elizabethan. If the Lord
released Will White, for the nonce, from the least
serious of his Puritan vows, Will Shakspere might
enjoy tilting a convivial glass with him as well
as with any living American. It came to me in
Emporia, not in the season of heat but of blazing
log-fires, when the yellow-gold leaves were drift-
ing down, and with them some flakes of early
Christmas snow, that my friend is a "merry gentleman," one who could both receive and return
a "God rest you."

I was living then, like the privileged, in the
upper chamber of the young and only daughter
of the family, who rode out joyously under the
elms on her horse one day and died. Mary was
sixteen, and, among her girlish treasures and her
grown-up books, her vital young head, her merry-
serious eyes, her thick childish pigtail were very
present to me. The day after she died, her father

gripped his feeling in his fist, leaned against his
Puritan backbone, and wrote of her in the *Gazette*
with a tender objectivity and clarity that made of
her obituary his classic. As I read, there sounded,
from the snowy air, the refrain of the Old English
carol:

> God rest you, merry gentlemen,
> May nothing you dismay.
> For Christ the Lord, our Saviour,
> Was born on Christmas Day.

# CHAPTER X

# PAUL ROBESON

*Man with his Home in a Rock*

PAUL ROBESON

*Camera Portrait by E. O. Hoppé*

# PAUL ROBESON

*Man with his Home in a Rock*

N the days of slavery Paul Robeson would have been one of the unknown and tragic creators of the Spirituals; a voice, rising out of the shadow, to wail for man's sins and sorrows, and urge a poignant resignation. His figure, always lithe and towering above his fellows, has a kind of haunted magnificence. Robeson is six feet two inches tall, and twenty-seven years old. The coppery brown of his skin takes the sheen of burnished metal. His powerfully moulded form, seen on the slave block in *The Emperor Jones,* is remembered like a Roman bronze of great period. But whether he appears in one of these disguises of the actor or in the conventional evening dress of a concert singer, the hearts of his audience respond. Here is a Black Boy who is sublimating the least acceptable of American destinies. When, in the first act of Tully's piece, that deep and gentle voice of primi-

tive innocence came out of the tattered figure of the Negro, the man beside me began to weep.

What can memories of savage freedom do for the civilized? Perhaps they can unify diverse gifts. Robeson's friendly dark face and strong, flexible body first became known to the press as those of a football hero. While still a student at Rutgers College, he made famous runs on Walter Camp's All-American team. Since 1924—his first notable appearance on the stage, in *All God's Chillun Got Wings*—and 1925—when he gave his first concert —he has won a conspicuous place for himself among American actors and singers. Yet, unlike most complex moderns, Paul Robeson does not appear half a dozen men in a torn and striving body. As a singer of Negro Spirituals, above all, he is one and clear-cut in the Greek or primordial sense.

This sureness of essential being takes him across the concert stage, as it did across the football field, with a fine, free movement of his athletic body, which is the reflection in action of an inward goal. Paul Robeson knows where he is bound, and has a confidence denied to most performers that his arms and legs will take him there with no conscious effort or control. When he turns back stage from an encore, one gets again, in the bend of his head, in the swift, diagonal line of his body, a sharp image from an old field of glory. The singer's

negroid features are intensified in a theatrical
light. His nose becomes a triangle of whiteness, his
eyes white moons, his skin takes a milky gleam. He
has never seen a Georgia road-gang, but when he
sings "Water Boy" the very accent and spirit of
the Negro labourers enter into him and come out
in the poignant vagrant song, one of the most
beautiful in all folk music. Yet I have never seen
on the stage a more civilized, a more finished artistic gesture than his nod to his accompanist, the
signal to begin the song. This gesture is the final
seal of Paul Robeson's personal ease in the world.

The primordial and early American world, with
all its stages from savagery to slavery and revolt
from slavery, to which he returned in the dream
visions and in the person of Brutus Jones, is Robeson's starting-point both as an actor and as a
singer. The basic tragedy of American life is his
tragedy: his own father was a slave. His ultimate
home is not Harlem or the Town Hall or the
Provincetown or the playhouses of London in
which he scored a great success, but that sure
spiritual haven where the sorrowing indignity and
the resignation of an oppressed race took their
refuge.

> I got a home in-a dat rock,
> Don't you see?

Robeson sings the phrase as an artist, aware of

the subtle correspondence between the hard *ck* sounds in "rock," and the firmness of Negro salvation, aware of the eloquence to his auditors of the deep, persuasive "don't you see?" But behind the artist, looking through his eyes, tightening his broad shoulders to bear a load of agonized entreaty, casting the outlines of his head into a sort of racial stereotype, solemnizing the tender reverberation of his voice, is an evangelical preacher, a seer, who, to reach the hearts of his clan, huddled in the southern wilderness, must out of the mystic and authoritative understanding of his own heart, sing his message.

This acceptance of the place where he stands as the place from which to start, instead of the place from which to escape, is the key to Robeson's history. He says that his father gave it to him in childhood, teaching him to live and work, not from the imitative or competitive racial base, as many intelligent Negroes have done, but merely to be *himself*, Paul Robeson, at his utmost stretch. Paul Robeson is a proud man. It was open to him, after his athletic victories at Rutgers and his double appearance on the All-American team, to be a professional athlete. Walter Camp called him "the greatest defensive end who ever trod the gridiron." He had the prize-fighter's physique and was mentioned for the ring. After his honours in debate and in scholarship at college—honours which would have been notable in a boy of any origin—he might have made a name in a learned profession: he holds a law degree from Columbia University. When these careers were renounced in favour of the life of the artist, there were still other choices. His singing voice is such a glorious and flexible organ and he has such an endearing stage presence that he might have been a star in coloured musical shows—he took the part of one of the "Four Harmony Kings" in *Shuffle Along* for a time. Had he chosen to cultivate his voice he might, perhaps, have made himself a concert singer of the type of Roland Hayes. But he told the London reporters recently that he did not aspire to sing opera airs except in the bath-tub. He has willed rather to be a serious actor and an evangelical and folk singer in the simple and naïve Negro tradition.

Paul Robeson is lucky, so they say, and one of his luckiest strikes is to have been born into the best age that the American Negro has yet known. But that is not saying much. Robeson, too, must have been made to feel at a disadvantage, as truly as his most humble brothers, by factors altogether beyond his control, if he had not learned to live so wisely on this American earth. The senior Robeson gave him something more abstract than a competitive ambition to strive for, and that in itself freed his power of choice. But his luck or his "leading" (as he sometimes calls it) seems to be in reality a blend of a tact—a highly sensitive intuition of the outer world—with a power to accept personal or racial limitations in a spirit of benignant grace and finality. This is the secret of the fortunate life that flows from Paul Robeson's whole person and quickens his audiences for a moment into the same finely tempered adjustment. Robeson's singing mouth has no twist of acrid pain. Notes of eternity roll out of it. They are round and whole. They come from the depths of a man who stands rooted in "the most ancient heavens."

George Jean Nathan, commenting on Paul Robeson's acting in *The Emperor Jones* and *All God's Chillun Got Wings,* described him as one of the most eloquent, impressive and convincing actors he had seen in twenty years of playgoing, and suggested that his college education had nothing to do with his flashes of blind inspiration, his power to wander on the borderline between acting and reality, his terrible and unrestrained sincerity. The Emperor's aboriginal voice, in the scene of lost and grovelling fear in the forest, made the hair of the civilized rise on their heads; they will not forget its sound to their dying day. It is true that Paul Robeson, even on the concert stage, seems sometimes to have the gift of possession. He himself does not know just how certain forces take control of his being—that self-denying, passive, deeply impressionable Negro essence which is a remarkable endowment for an artist of the stage, much of whose skill must rest on his power of self-immolation or identification. Yet, knowing Paul Robeson, one is bound to believe that "education" has shared the honours with inheritance in his life story. If what lies below the surface is struggling for expression in an ignorant primitive mind, it is likely to come out in a less manageable form than art, or in an art that lacks even a bowing acquaintance with opportunity. The stability and happiness given to a black boy's formative years by success in a rounded existence, where he lived on terms of affection and comradeship with the white people of his world, undoubtedly helped to make Paul Robeson articulate. Success and self-confidence, necessary as daily bread to the dramatic temper, were the soil in which the unconscious stream of tradition, which now serves his art so well, could grow and mature.

Princeton, New Jersey, might not seem as good a place as some southern town for an exponent of Negro tradition to be born in, but here again Robeson was lucky. Princeton is neither north nor south, and for a Negro boy in his time had the advantages of both. Paul's mother was a schoolteacher and a Bustill of Philadelphia—that is to say, a woman of an "old Philadelphia" coloured family, who prided herself on her birth and background. His father, the Rev. William Robeson, who had escaped at fifteen from the south and from slavery, put himself through Lincoln University and became a Methodist minister, was of pure black stock, probably very close to the African. The people of the North Carolina community from which he came are said to have been of the Bantu tribe. Simple relatives on the paternal side, following the minister from North Carolina to Princeton, became in a sort Paul's female guardians after the death of his mother. The loss came when he was very young, and this southern clan might still, as far as culture went, have been living in a primitive rural community. The same could be said of the simple folk of his father's congregation in Somerville, New Jersey, whither the elder Robeson moved three years later. When Paul sang the Spirituals and work songs of his race with his aunts and cousins or with his father's parishioners, he was living and feeling wholly in the old Negro mode. As he was at the same time working ambitiously in white schools, his existence enacted itself on two entirely different levels. It is a fact—though few of the dominant race have the imagination to realize it—that the life of a Negro, or an Indian, or even a Russian Jew, must always be lived in the United States on two planes. This double existence too often creates below the surface a deadly war of shame and blame. In Paul's case, by one of the miracles that create fine personalities and destinies, specifically by the influence of a far-seeing old man, the two planes were assimilable and friendly one with the other; they even intercommunicated.

If Paul Robeson were to write the autobiography of these early years he would surely call it *Father and Son*. The image of a tall, grizzled, commanding evangelist with a magnificent bass voice ("When people talk about my voice," says Robeson, "I wish they could have heard my father preach"), a father who was old enough to be a grandfather, an earnest and loving religious presence, will always stand by him through life. Paul was the youngest of a sizable family, already launched in the world, and so it came about that this close and tender companionship, which any father might envy, and any son covet, grew up between the two. When Paul sings that touching song which has in it so much of the fate of the coloured race:

> Sometimes I feel like a motherless child
> A long ways from home,

I seem to see the two faces, the old and the young, engaged in their serious colloquies. Before the move from Princeton there had been troubles in the church. The resignation of the minister fol-

lowed, and some of Paul's childish memories concern his father's conduct under fire, his dignity
and lack of bitterness, which became to the son a
sort of pattern of the ideal human attitude, especially the ideal Negro attitude. The human love,
the religious simplicity and pathos that he brings
to his singing of the Spirituals are a direct heritage,
and he ascribes to the influences of these years his
ability to pour himself freely and fearlessly into
his professional work to-day, as he poured himself
freely into his work in school and college.

The father, of course, had no thought of an
artistic career for his son. He destined Paul—
whose elder brothers and sister were already
headed for superior professions as doctor, minister, teacher—first for the ministry; then, as the
boy rebelled, for the law. Paul's intelligence justi-
fied his hopes. The lad's progress was brilliant; one
victory followed another, scholarly, oratorical,
athletic. When he came home from school, the father would say: "Now tell me what you learned in
Latin to-day." Not only every lesson but every
debate, every football match, was rehearsed to a
critic whose understanding and pride were a spur
to solid performance. When Paul brought back
seven A's and one B from his freshman examina-
tions at college, his father inquired: "What's the
idea of the B?" If Paul Robeson can get seven A's
he can get eight. Paul agreed. So he led his class

in scholarship, won his Phi Beta Kappa key in his junior year, became a brilliant debater, and achieved a varsity letter in five sports and a place on the coveted "All-American."

The cross which every Negro bears was not wholly lifted from Paul Robeson's shoulders. Thorns pricked through his victories, and the moment came when he, too, had to take his place on one side or the other of the colour line. At the gate of Columbia, with a law degree in his hand, and the door of an excellent New York law office opening before him he hesitated. All Negroes are mariners, and it is so I see Paul Robeson holding his sensitive compass to the New York wind. Nothing in life had led him to fear white competition in the concrete instance, for he had always been at the head of any white group where he found himself. Yet the needle still pointed to the black pole of the Negro. His "advantages" had not made it veer by one degree from that fixed point. "In the law I could never reach the peak: I could never be a Supreme Court judge: on the stage there was only the sky to hold me back." How much shrewd judgment, how much new hope and emotional drive behind these words!

By this time Paul Robeson knew his race. He saw some among its leaders who had made their way by the road of revolt and bitterness, with the lash of a dark hatred on their backs. He saw still others who had proved their ability to equal white men on sophisticated cultural ground, and who urged him in strong accents to move forward in this course, "to show them what you can do." These motives seemed to him small and mean. He had no use for colour as a weapon, but he felt a great expansion of the soul when he saw the young Negroes, as he did all about him in Harlem, seeking the way, not of race abnegation or of race rivalry, but of race consciousness. The Negro Renascence! The phrase was life-giving! So far as it was a fact, and not a hope or an intellectual formulation, it rested on the free development of Negro characteristics and cultural resources. Through the evocations of poetry, the provocations of jazz, through the theatre, through folk music, the Negro was coming into his American rights at last and offering his treasure to the common store.

Paul Robeson, being a Negro, wanting to be one to the limit, knowing already an unusual degree of personal success and expressiveness, discerned then that he could best continue to achieve them in the realm of the arts. Why had he studied law? Not so much because he loved it as because it seemed the highest destiny he could choose. Well, he had now seen a higher, and knew intuitively that he had a genius for it. He was a natural artist, and a fabricated attorney after all. This new opportunity was in line with the spirit of the elder Robeson, because it forced Paul to look within for strength. Some courage was needed to cast aside financial security and years of specialized training for the rigours and uncertainties of the artist's life. But if the artist, more than any other, must lose his life to find it, so must the American Negro be born twice into the American universe to live there like a man. In Paul Robeson man and artist now met and voted to take their daily sufferings, their daily nightmare fears, their daily soaring ambitions in common.

So began the second arc of Paul Robeson's mounting career. In this arc of his maturity, which is only half traced as yet, he has found a seconder as devoted as his father to provide the security and spur that his gentle nature demands. Paul Robeson married, the summer of his graduation from the Law School, a brilliant girl of Spanish coloured extraction. Eslanda Goode, a chemist by training, gave up a responsible post in the pathological laboratory of the Presbyterian Hospital to become her husband's manager. He might not have been the first—as he has—to bring his folk music to the concert platform as a subject for an entire program by a single artist if he had not found a backer in this strong young woman. Yet God Almighty was Robeson's greatest backer from the start. He gave him his simple and beloved personality and his voice, so dusky and so mellow, with its elemental power of leading men to springs of tragic truth. The images that hardened newspaper critics use to describe this voice are telling: "It has organ notes." "It is a voice in which deep bells ring." "It is like the wind in the tree-tops." "It has restraint and power which hold thunder behind each song." "It compasses some universal tragedy of the spirit."

The public felt the quality both of Robeson's singing and speaking voice in his first serious stage performance—a rather mediocre Negro play called *Voodoo,* which nevertheless, in a harking back to the savage past, somewhat reminiscent of *The Emperor Jones,* gave the actor a chance to show the natural and simple power of his art. Robeson played the rôle in England, with Mrs. Patrick Campbell, after the New York performance, and began to lay the foundations of the success of esteem and popularity which he achieved there later in *The Emperor Jones*. His New York performance in the same rôle was of course contrasted with that of Gilpin, who first created the rôle. To some minds, Gilpin gave a less "intelligent" but a more effectively wicked performance, especially of the rascally first act. Those who most admire Robeson as a singer do not always esteem him to the same degree as an actor. But he found many warm critical admirers and in London was named a foredestined Othello. As Jim, the Christ-like Negro husband of the white girl who loses her mind, in O'Neill's much discussed play of racial intermarriage, he had a rarely sensitive tragic part.

Robeson's voice is described as a "bass-baritone." It has pace and enunciation and has been well placed and cultivated just enough—not too much —for the faithful adherence to primitive tradition. Robeson's rendering of the Spirituals, with the expert and exciting accompaniment and transcription or Mr. Lawrence Brown, is less etherealized than that of Roland Hayes, technically speaking a much more finished artist. But Robeson's seems to contain more of the background, more of the associations both in a racial and a musical sense, more of the artless majesty of the originals. These Spirituals, primarily intended for choral singing, are, as James Weldon Johnson points out, a high test of the individual performer, who must render not only the melodies but in his accompaniment the harmonies, and in addition convey undertones and overtones that can never be transcribed at all. Robeson's interpretation has no lapses into the jazzed effects and the Russian harmonies that have recently crept into the Spirituals, both in stage and in choral singing. It is a "classic" interpretation, strictly within Negro tradition, yet owes the subtlest of its beauties to a personal and temperamental inheritance. "Witness," for instance, may be sung as by a member of the congregation. Robeson sings it as a preacher. His evangelical father is never far from his shoulder. The Spirituals with an element of comedy, like "Scandalize My Name" are very much less his forte than the songs of plaintive and tender dependence, or vigorous exhortation.

Paul Robeson the fine actor, playing the stringent dramas of modernity; Paul Robeson the singer, working consciously and lovingly in an unconscious folk art, clarifying it so that white men may make it—as Europeans have made their folk-songs—the basis of a sophisticated musical expression: he is a symbol of the New Age of the Negro, a figure of our year and hour. Yet even in this hour, when the Black Man is the fashion, when operas and ballets are jazzed, when he himself is playing night after night in a Broadway theatre, this Afro-American, with his prize-fighter's build, his trained intelligence, his artistic aspiration, his gentle evangelical heart, does not walk too easily about New York. Watch him in the subway, reading some critical musical work from the Harlem Public Library, and you will see the winds of doubt assail him. O'Neill has showed us some of the ways in which the Negro may not achieve happiness, and we shall be witness to others, on the stage and off, as the races mingle and wrestle. But Robeson on the stage, and especially when he sings—when his voice, released from inhibition, flows up and out from some darkly crystalline spring, seems to be meeting Happiness face to face.

In the bottom of the spring is a treasure—the treasure of chastened hope which the humble have laid away. Feathery tree branches are reflected in the water, and one sees the wavering image of little Negro cabins, where bald old men and crooning women commune with eternity. Beside the spring is a great rock—the rock, remote from the clashing ambitions of New York, where Robeson the artist has his home. I am grateful that I have seen the shadow of the rock, and in the rush of the water heard a kind of Negro Chaliapin, who is yet a Black Boy, singing the Spirituals with wildness and awe, like a trusting child of God.

# CHAPTER XI

# ALICE HAMILTON

*Scientist in Armour*

# ALICE HAMILTON

*Scientist in Armour*

LICE HAMILTON—an old-fashioned Scotch-Irish name. Can you see the woman who owns it—a lady in the early fifties with dusky black hair turned grey, hazel eyes serene and searching, profile of a classic gravity and purity—moving quietly about a square New England house that rises high among its elms above a wide, slow-flowing river, where a little ferry of grandfatherly cut plies unhurriedly from shore to shore? Frame the picture in carved walnut, scratch the delicate lines and shadows of the gentle, withdrawn face in dry-point, and you will have one aspect—the retired, domestic, Victorian—of the leading American expert in one of the newest fields of scientific medicine: a doctor who by an original combination of gifts has been able to mitigate the danger of the lives on which American industry rests.

So, opposite the Hadlyme picture you must set

another—or rather a reel of pictures that unwinds itself north and south, east and west, across the United States: a slender, tweed-clad figure walking intrepidly on narrow planks hundreds of feet above the ground beside vats of seething sulphuric acid; dropping down vertical ladders into the dense darkness of copper mines; crawling on hands and knees into remote stopes; listening in back rooms of saloons or union headquarters to strange tales in halting foreign tongues; listening with equal attention in polished offices to the fluent statistics of captains of industry. It has been Doctor Hamilton's fate in her public, humane, and scientific rôle to live the very opposite of the secluded life which her personal atmosphere seems to demand. Laboratories, settlements, mine corridors, factories, international congresses, medical schools, lecture platforms—in such tense centres of modern group life where human beings are struggling and striving together for pathological discovery, for social amelioration, for material and economic conquest and gain, for international understanding, have her best years been passed. In the interest of her special researches into occupational disease she has gone everywhere that a man could go—never considering herself a woman when it came to danger or fatigue—and to many where no male scientist would have wished to penetrate—never considering herself an "expert," with a dignity that must be preserved, when it came to sitting in the kitchen of a Mexican miner's wife.

Alice Hamilton is thus known and loved by many kinds and conditions of Americans. But the general public has barely heard of her—much less, for instance, than of her friends and associates of many years at Hull-House, Jane Addams and Julia Lathrop. She is by training a reticent scientist, and has never dramatized either her subject or her mission, though the former is highly sensational, lurid enough to provide thrillers for an adventure magazine. It isn't easy to make her give herself away. When asked by a designing relative what compliment had pleased her most, she answered: "In a metallurgical magazine a smelting expert wrote: 'Here is a woman writing on the metallurgy of lead who knows her job perfectly.'" And she added that, if she were successful in her work, it was because she always learned all there was to know about every trade before she began to make her visits to the plants. This feeling for the technic of a profession, artistic or scientific, as you like, has made Doctor Hamilton's work at least as well known and valued in European countries whose "unprogressiveness" many Americans despise—but where human life is nevertheless held dear and its protection carefully assured—as in the land of the free.

This doctor is the woman in American public life whom I should wish to present to a scientific Frenchman; if only to prove to him that in a country where professional women are borrowing hard and objective qualities from the other sex, there is one lady of the old school who has made an exquisite and easy adjustment to both sides of life—the tough and the tender, the hard work and the human relations—without sacrificing the virtues of either. "Wine, silver, and homespun," said Walter Lippmann of Alice Hamilton. She has neither renounced her inborn graciousness nor used it ignobly, and her mellow cultivation, her æsthetic sensibility, her fine, exact, smooth-working mind, her perfect simplicity and humbleness of character, her honesty of speech tempered with consideration, her complete competence in her subject, would fill a Frenchman with respect.

But if he wished to know (as he would) why it is to this quiet woman more than to any scientist of the other sex that we owe the beginnings of our growing, if still imperfect, knowledge of the horrible forms of disease, dissolution, and death which modern industry has sown like dragons' teeth across the United States, I should ask him to listen to Doctor Hamilton's voice. A rich voice, drawing much, like her face and presence, from the generation behind, but with undertones of pity and irony which float out like harp notes when the springs of compassion are touched. The poignant notes—though they may have echoes of an ancient Irish tale of sorrow and revolt—seem born of the agony and fury of an age that values machines and their products: material objects like steel rails, smokeless powder, lead paint, knockless gasoline—before the brief and tender lives of men.

In H. G. Wells's novel, Doctor Devizes, the modern scientist, sums up his personal philosophy to Christina Alberta, the modern girl, in terms that Alice Hamilton might well subscribe to: "I do not want to be a brilliant person. I want to be a vital part." And then, "You'll never run parallel with men, you free women," he continues. "You've got to work out a way that is different. Different down to the roots." This was certainly not the creed of most of our early suffrage and educational leaders. It is not that of the Woman's Party to-day, nor yet of most of the women who have a share in the regular political parties. These types of feminists have frankly worked for parallelism and for power. Their inward urge to bring women exactly to men's level, to extend feminine sway through the sharing of male "rights," provided a potent force at a time when high explosives were in order. But the young woman of the hour, coming into her vote, her college, and her job as if God had given them to her has more to learn from Alice Hamilton's life than from that of Susan B. Anthony or Anna Howard Shaw. Alice Hamilton, too, is a pioneer, but with a difference. A sprig of the younger branch of that first ardent generation of feminists which was suddenly impelled—or was it compelled? to grow away from the sedate domestic tree, she has remained sedate in the Jane Austen sense. She looks at men, as objective feminine beings always have, amusedly, tolerantly, affectionately, and without ire. Even with a feeling that they are "superior." The intellectual and detached aspects of her mind have unconsciously served the more instinctive feminine creature, and the latter has skilfully managed to make her a persuasive rather than an assertive innovator; a conservationist; a guardian of the race.

One thing she could not do, perhaps because she was brought up in a pioneer community; stop pioneering. The chair she occupies at the Harvard Medical School was created for her, immediately after the war, and she is, so far, the only woman to be invited to that conservative medical faculty. She was the first woman investigator for the Federal Department of Labor in the field of poisonous industries. Her book on Industrial Poisons, a weighty scientific work, not a popular treatise, was in its background derived from these venturesome studies. Yet it is as if honours and attainments meant nothing to her in themselves, nothing as objectives. How lightly she holds them— how differently from the way men—and feminists—hold honours! They have not been Alice Hamilton's life, only by-products of her life. An Irish heart, impatient and humane, a cool, definite mind seeking primarily knowledge, not conflict or domination: these were her endowment. Slowly the two matured, slowly they joined forces and out of piercing conviction sought, crusader-like, to share their knowledge and make their wisdom prevail.

But when Alice Hamilton left the genteel shelter of Miss Porter's boarding-school at Farmington, Connecticut, for a mid-western co-educational medical college, it was far from her thought or ambition to seek a position of authority in American industry, and an Assistant Professorship of Industrial Medicine at Harvard University. Even now she must often wonder to herself how in the world it came about that a girl brought up in Fort Wayne, Indiana, by a father interested only in poetry and history and free discussion, and a mother interested only in modern languages and fresh air, should have turned into an expert in lead processes, and become, in her maturity, a sort of special adviser and ambassador to the "hardest-boiled," the most practical and unimaginative set of men in these United States.

Alice Hamilton's Scotch-Irish grandfather

came to his small Indiana town as a young man, and gradually the large Hamiltonian clan assembled about him: a distinguished, vivacious group of cousins, whose rich and carefully articulated speech and highly intellectual atmosphere suggested foreign origins. Moreover, Alice Hamilton's father and her mother, who was an eastern woman, did not believe in schooling. "We were expected," writes Margaret, one of Alice's sisters, now of the Bryn Mawr School of Baltimore (every member of this family of four sisters and one brother, by the way, has been connected with education), "to *know* literature—French, German, and English—to know history by reading all the many books about us. One did not study these subjects; they were to be read and enjoyed. Modern languages were learned by conversation and reading. Latin and mathematics were our only lessons. This curious method of education made for hard work on our part. We were determined to be educated. It made for independence of mind, as we had to answer our own questions, solve our own problems. Alice remembers one task set her by her father, when she was fourteen years old— to seek what proof of the doctrine of the Trinity she could find in the Bible. Her first piece of research! We heard all the topics of the day discussed: Free Trade, England and Expansion, the Democratic Party. We learned to fight for our education. All interest, all excitement in our restricted small-town life came to us through books and ideas."

This type of education would naturally have led Alice Hamilton into pure science; and it was, in fact, her starting-point, in spite of her halt at Farmington. One of her school-mates there remembers the impression made upon the more worldly New Yorkers, whose heads were full of husbands and "coming out," when lovely (though a bit countrified) young Alice, with her melting Irish looks, declared in her deep, clear voice her ambition to "go everywhere and know all sorts of people, maybe as a medical missionary to Persia or maybe in the slums of New York or both," but never to settle down till she had seen the world of men. She herself thinks that her choice of a career was almost accidental. She and her sister Edith, who shared her "finishing" at Miss Porter's, decided that they wanted "a larger life," and that it could come only through a profession. There were but two openings for women at that time, teaching and medicine. But teaching was restricted to one *milieu* and perhaps one sex, and Alice wanted something more. So she elected medicine and entered the school of the University of Michigan at twenty-one. From there she went to Germany to study bacteriology and pathology, and thence to what she describes as the most exciting year of her life—an interneship at the old-fashioned New England Hospital for women in Boston. It was her first adventure in an American city, her first contact—through the clinic—with poor working-people.

One of her fellow internes, a Russian woman, who later also became associated with Hull-House, describes the surprising arrival in the prim corridors of the hospital of "a very, *very* pretty young girl," accompanied by a young man whom she affectionately kissed good-bye, under the shocked eye of the stodgy women doctors. "My cousin"—the Hamiltonian pronunciation of the word seems to elevate it for the ear into a sort of royalty. The most striking thing about this quaint young interne, so modest and so unsophisticated, and yet, after all, so sure, was her "desire to know." "*Tell me everything*"—over and over she insisted, as if the need to understand and to penetrate others' lives and points of view was essential. And what she came to know about the varieties of human experience by this power of identification which was at once objective and sympathetic, she *accepted* with tolerance—however at variance from her own thought and habit. Add to her discovery of the fascination of human beings in the clinic and the hospital, a passion, newly discovered, too, for babies, for any babies, however sick or dirty; a revolt against benighted elders; and a clear-cut vision that she did not want to practise medicine because of the responsibilities for human life involved; and you have the substance of Alice Hamilton's year as an interne.

Next she accepted a teaching position at the Women's Medical School of Northwestern University in Chicago, applying, simultaneously, for a residence at Hull-House. The latter step was final. Once taken, the logic of her destiny was inescapable. The settlement was about eight years old at this time, and already so famous that Alice Hamilton was convinced that it could not accept so insignificant a unit as herself. Yet an irresistible desire drove her to join Jane Addams, in her then revolutionary job. If the psychologists are right in maintaining that our lives move in inevitable repetitions of the same cycle, established by our early years, it seems that Alice Hamilton, in entering Hull-House, was in a sense returning to an enlargement of that big, discursive, and somewhat feminized pioneer family where she had grown up. Here, too, were a remarkable group of independent women and a few clever, high-minded men; here were sustaining and varied friendships that came very close to the rounded human family life; here was acute and radical discussion on every controversial subject. Hull-House added the same thing that Alice Hamilton had found in her Boston clinic—an intense and humane concern for people who have small chance in this world. Books and ideas abounded in that sober background of Morris browns and greens, but the chief interest of the residents came through a different channel.

The young doctor took no vows when she entered Hull-House, but her special duty as a resident was to wash Italian babies in the basement on Saturday mornings—the only day when she did not teach—and she frankly says that nothing she has done before or since has given her so much satisfaction. In addition, she experimented with infant feeding, and gradually took on the task (one that no doctor of the stronger sex would have imagined) of herself conducting the sick children to hospitals and dispensaries. In short, she developed a sort of child health centre at a time when there was no such institution in Chicago, and no social service in hospitals. Yet there was never any question of her abandoning her own scientific line in favour of "pure settlement work." She was conscientious in her teaching, and when she left Northwestern, went, in 1903, to the Memorial Institute for Infectious Diseases, where, under Dr. Ludwig Hektoen, she undertook serious scientific research.

Doctor Hektoen respected this young woman's approach. She made the utmost of the problem in hand; her results were clear, complete, logical, well arranged, reinforced by her power of wide scientific reading in foreign tongues and fields. Her first research was on typhoid, her problem being to get actual confirmation of the then un-proved hypothesis that flies carry typhoid bacilli. This work, done in connection with the practical study of one thousand homes in the Hull-House district, where an epidemic was raging at the time, and where specimen flies were carefully collected for the scientists in the tenements, had highly suc-cessful results, both pragmatic and scientific: the problem was proved and the district and the city administration were "cleaned up."

But Alice Hamilton was coming to realize that "pure research" was not a field in which she could hope to make a contribution important enough to compensate for the abnegation of human rela-tionships. She knew that she was more a member of Miss Addams's family than she was a teacher or a research worker. The emotional centre of her life was not in a laboratory or a class room. The hu-man need at Hull-House in the days of its strenu-ous youth was inescapable. One of the Italian girls whom she unsewed from her swaddling clothes many years ago used to me of her friend the very words of the fellow interne: "Ever since I was a baby she has *wanted to know* everything—just everything; when she comes back now, the first thing, she takes you up to her room and makes you tell everything—how your job is, and about the

boys, and all about your sinus and your family."
And there were many neighbourhood problems
more pressing than Francesca's—for example, desperate evidence of the casual methods of American industry. Alice Hamilton remembers the feelings of anger and revolt with which she used to
pass the unregenerate Pullman factory of those
days.

And then an English book, Sir Thomas Oliver's
*Dangerous Trades,* came into her hands and provided the key for which she had been half consciously waiting. The industrial poisons which
Oliver described and the damage they were doing
to working-people must be as common in America as in Europe. They were going on, unchecked
and unregarded, at the very gates of Hull-House.
So does a great opportunity crystallize in a thunder clap, with a lightning flash of insight. Alice
Hamilton could never wonder again where lay
her path as a medical pioneer. It stretched before
her: she was to use the findings of pathological
science to better, not in a vaguely altruistic, but
in a concrete, scientific way, the daily lives and
serious medical ills of working men and women.

The opening came very quickly. A commission
was appointed to study the industrial diseases of
the state of Illinois. Alice Hamilton was its special
investigator. She made a study of all the industries of the state using lead and arsenic, and Hull-

House, which loves the conquest of evil, sharpened its vibrant, determined group effort into a shield and buckler for her labours. Alice Hamilton is a thoroughly independent spirit, but not naturally a speaker or a propagandist. She became one only because she must, and she was lucky in having at her side in Hull-House two friends who were also remarkable social generals, Jane Addams, a great humane leader and founder of causes, and Julia Lathrop—later first head of the Children's Bureau—a woman of terse and salty humour and keen political insight. A state law—the first in the country for the protection of workers in poisonous industries—was passed in Illinois as a result of the findings of the commission. But before that happened, Alice Hamilton had found the inevitable extension of her opportunity, through the startled illumination of the United States Commissioner of Labor. This was in the year 1910. Mr. Neil was attending an International Congress on Industrial Hygiene at Brussels. An American woman doctor, a quiet person, very sure of her facts and courageous in stating them, was reading a paper. The Commissioner discovered that his country was years behind all the civilized world in its knowledge of the dangers of industry, and of the ways of protecting the workers against them. The woman scientist evidently already knew something about the subject.

227

She was invited to become an employee of the Department of Labor.

For the next eleven years—until the Harding Administration—Doctor Hamilton remained a servant of the government. Her residence at Hull-House has been only partial ever since, though it has remained the home of her spirit. She could go back there, and still does, to write the reports of her investigations, which took her into almost every industrial centre in the country and almost every state. The very catalogue of her researches is staggering, and reveals the abyss of insecurity on which our American civilization rests—since our houses and their fixtures, our clothes, our heat, our light, our motor-cars, our newspapers, points of stability on a whirling planet, are points of acute danger for the lives that produce them.

The study of lead occupied the first five years of research: white and red lead, smelting and refining, glazing and decorating pottery and tiles, enamelling bath-tubs and sinks, the painter's trade, the printer's trade, manufacture of storage batteries, compounding rubber. From 1916, when the speeding up of munitions for the Allies began, until the Armistice, she studied explosive and shell plants and airplane works using poisonous dope. After the Armistice new and important aniline dye works brought new dangers. Carbon-monoxide gassing in steel-mills and coal-mines claimed attention. Along with her Harvard professorship—which presumably grew out of the war and the increased interest in the lives of workmen—she has continued to make numerous independent investigations; as of mercurial poison. Felt hats and thermometers may cost dear! But the mercury-miners of California are no more interesting to her than the granite-cutters of Vermont, or the potters of New Jersey.

It was a queer sort of job that Doctor Hamilton had in the government service: the Department of Labor had no authority to send her into any plant. She had to make her way by tact, persuasion, intuitive imagination. Moreover, no data existed to tell her what poisons were in use or where. The European literature, so valuable on the physiological side, did not bridge the differences between European and American technique. Trades that were dangerous there proved not to be so here, and the reverse. Hospital records did not supply the gaps. Not one American hospital in twenty keeps the records that are needed by the industrial toxicologist, and the sickness insurance system, which in Europe automatically brings to light the incidence of illness of all kinds, among all types of workers, does not exist on our individualistic shores. In short, the information Alice Hamilton was seeking was "nobody's business."

Nobody's business has always been woman's business, but only a mind with a power of hard, exact thought and a drive of adventurous curiosity could have made woman capable of this. The clinical picture and the pathological data were in a doctor's province. But I marvel that such a vast number of complex technical processes, devised by the brilliant collaboration of engineers and chemists, should store themselves like so many lyric poems in a gentle Victorian head. Doctor Hamilton is a passionate traveller. If you take a journey with her in the United States, she will recognize from the train every factory that is belching steam at the sky, and, abandoning her serene restraint for a kind of Godwinian fervour, tell you exactly what is going on, for good or ill, within its walls.

It was not as a critic, it was as a scientist, however, that she began and continued her studies. The industrialists were genuinely bewildered by any hint of criticism. In the days of her first studies they had never thought of their industries as of public concern. Their business was their "private property." Few employers were really callous, though one did assure her that he never used lead in the manufacture of bath-tubs and displayed work-rooms where leadless paint was used on the outsides of the tubs—concealing those where the insides were enamelled in a terrible lead atmosphere. Others, and these were the majority, were ready and eager to improve conditions, provided she could give them the weight of evidence. But they were realists and they all "had to be shown."

She tells a story of a lead plant where conditions were peculiarly outrageous, the air thick with white lead dust; no facilities for washing, no lunch rooms. The superintendent, who was taking her about, perceiving her distress, said consolingly: "Well, we've got one place here you'll like"—and he conducted her to a luxurious white-tiled stable, full of sleek animals. "There's nothing," he said, "Mr. Blank wouldn't do for his horses." Yet even Mr. Blank, when the true conditions of his industrial workers were revealed to him, made all the changes that the doctor suggested. "Showing" has been Alice Hamilton's long suit.

Yet the difficulty of obtaining accurate data is immense. What conferences she has had with humble foreign doctors—company doctors, she soon found, are often unwilling to give out facts which may be damaging—apothecaries, visiting nurses, charity workers, undertakers, priests! The most important information has naturally come direct from the workers, and no saloon and no tenement have been too sordid for her to penetrate.

The foreign-born workers and union officials

were primarily as suspicious as the employers. She
has won their confidence—as she did that of the
owners—by her sympathy and her true neutrality
and her expert capacity. I can see a workman of
forty, shrivelled into the aspect of eighty by lead-
poisoning, telling her his whole story. I can see
the sunburnt, stringy mine owners in wild western towns describing to a charming lady of the
old school, welcomed like royalty at their table,
their investment of strenuous labour and capital,
and revealing the constructive imagination which
made their ventures possible. In a subject in which
nobody, it seems, can be impartial—where apple
pie and late hours are blamed for lead-poisoning
and all employers are devils—she has managed not
to antagonize either side; and so to make protective measures possible, and save many lives. The
greatest tribute to her mental integrity came during the war, when, in spite of her avowed and
fervent pacifism, her study of munition plants for
the Department of Labor was unquestioned.

Doctor Hamilton's quiet work has had its effect. The more progressive states have gradually
passed protective legislation and the public is no
longer wholly in blinders. But the ill-disposed em-
ployer, he that "values things more than life,"
can often get round the law; and no state or federal agency has both power and expert knowledge
to keep track of these swift-springing, death-

dealing poisons, whose alphabetical names twist the tongue. So the fate of the American workman rests still with the individual owner—with him and with the indefatigable detached scientist like Alice Hamilton. It was she, of course, who rose in a stormy Congress where many business interests were involved and urged that if England was able, in war-time, to discontinue airplane processes which proved prejudicial to health, Americans should in learning how to take the knock out of gasoline take time enough not to kill workingmen by the way. Somehow, her earnest, unsentimental, courageous, forthright speeches manage to convey, as surely as the bowed head of a Mater Dolorosa, a sense of the preciousness of human life. "Stop a minute," the undertones command. "These statistics I am giving you are not marks on paper: they are men and women, fragile creatures of flesh and blood. See what you are greedily and needlessly destroying."

Alice Hamilton's schoolgirl desire to "go everywhere, know all sorts of people, and never settle down until she had seen the world of men" has been completely fulfilled. She knows our country intensively and widely, our flat, sun-gilded western deserts no less than our electric city-streets. The mechanical heart-beats of the plants that our human heart-beats are striving so hard to keep up with are the rhythm she breathes to, and the grovelling foreign populations they secrete are her friends. What a fierce internationalist and pacifist she has been! This "subject" of hers, which is from one aspect a collection of cold statistics, and from another a modernist painting, built up in strange angular lines and smirched with lurid, discordant colours—she has studied its development in eight countries of Europe and has even seen the textile mills of Japan, full of patient little yellow people. Always she has pierced through barriers, to "the inside." Is there a door in the world that will not open to her quiet sympathetic question? She always manages to touch life, as a doctor should, where it is raw and bleeding. In 1915 she went through the warring countries of Europe with Jane Addams, in the interest of neutral arbitration, and later conferred at Zurich with The League for Peace, which had German and Austrian women among its delegates. In 1919, shortly after the Treaty, with the same companion, she studied the effect of starvation on the Germans for Hoover and the Quakers, and she has since visited Bolshevik Russia, at the invitation of the Department of Health, to study the control of industrial disease. She is the only woman member on the Health Committee of the League of Nations.

What has driven so fast and so far a lady of demure and comely habit? A heart, I imagine,

whose fires, like the magic fires in the blast-
furnaces, are ever burning, a heart that had to live
dangerously and yet was forced to express itself
in the rigorous terms of science. Alice Hamilton
is rigorous. She has never asked life to give her
comfort—a pioneer who grew up close to untouched solitudes of lake and plain and forest has
no right to it, she would say—but she has insisted
that life in giving her its accurate unlovely facts
should add a dash of wild natural beauty. She
might have been a painter, they tell me. That may
be why I think of her walking alone on a path by
a flowing river, on some October evening when
the New England air and sky are crisp and luminous. From the old house behind her—homespun,
familiar, and gentle, with its lighted lamps—come
the mellow, disputatious voices of the Hamilton
sisters—and their "cousins." But here in the night
the stars prick the sumach leaves and the current
washes softly on the bank. This is the atmosphere,
fine, sharp, austere, from which a modern cru-
sader, tempered by life but every year more un-
resigned, draws spirit and health for the next vital
study of the diseases of modernity.

# CHAPTER XII

# H. L. MENCKEN

*"He Must and Will be Titan."*

H. L. MENCKEN

*Camera Portrait by E. O. Hoppé*

# H. L. MENCKEN

*"He Must and Will be Titan"*

OMING towards me, very swiftly, as I walked in the direction of Fifth Avenue on Forty-fourth Street, I saw a rather short, stocky figure of a man, whose blue eyes shone ahead of him like a sort of searchlight. He leaned a little forward, stooping his shoulders, as if to hasten his pace, and he was strongly careened to the right: a boat under full sail. But what bore him down and forward was not a spanking breeze; it was an obviously weighty travelling-bag, suspended from a long and almost Simian arm. This pedestrian seemed more alertly intent on his way and his business than any other man within range: those chinablue eyes were not preoccupied with Forty-fourth Street at all, but with some inner objective toward which they were heading. It struck me with a shade of surprise that a prosperous bourgeois American should be carrying his own handbag,

instead of voyaging in a taxi. So, as he passed, I took rather special notice of a short, square, pleasant, determined face. The man was in his prime, yet there was something boyish about him. He belonged to the business world, yet there was something of the thinker in his mien. He was very much at home in New York—indeed, I thought I had seen him before myself—yet he had the air of a visitor. A provincial professor of some very living subject, on his way to a congress? I fear I have spoken an insult. For the man I had noted was H. L. Mencken, *en route* from Hollins Street, Baltimore, via the caves of the Heckscher Building, to the Hotel Algonquin.

I tracked him down at last, you see, in Alfred Knopf's waiting-room. As I sat somnolently on a deep couch, in the shaded light, Mencken was dismissing, very kindly, a young aspirant who would have liked to be told exactly how to write his article for the *American Mercury*. Mencken knows his influence with the youth of the age, and it has reached his ears that the writers in his magazine are prone to imitate him. He explained that he had made it a rule to know nothing about any article until it reached his desk, in finished form. So dismissing, he collided with a tall glass vase of red flowers. The vase fell over; young ladies with bobbed hair came running at the crash. Mencken was for a moment aghast. He made sounds and gestures of compunction and dismay. Then he came to himself: "Anyhow it was an ugly vase," he said, with that blue-eyed laugh which has something remote and mirthless about it, vanishing in the direction of his private lair, while the secretaries picked up the pieces.

But he does not wish to be thought of as a "slayer." So he told me, very earnestly, on another occasion, in his rooms at the Algonquin, after an absinthe cocktail had been dispensed, and a perfect bottle of Moselle placed handy, and a well-chosen jellied bird—this befell on a hot summer day—set on the board. He need not have said it, for even in these impersonal hotel rooms, he moves in an atmosphere of amenity. Only a gentle host, in the old-fashioned sense, a host who is also an artist—and surely artists are seldom slayers, at bottom—could take so much trouble about gastronomy and vintages. I had expected to meet an artist and an epicure, but I was hardly prepared for the sentimentalist—the solid, Germanic sentimentalist—who emerged when he talked of Baltimore, its stable and familiar scenes: the red brick house with white trimmings where he had lived for forty-odd years; the quiet domestic life that has gone on there; the classical orchestral music that is produced by the Saturday Night Club, where, with a group of tried old friends, doctors and professors, Mencken plays the second piano part. Even when Mencken is "slaying," it is, I think, to the great roll of the Eroica. In his daily friendly intercourse, one hears another, less fateful, more fitful strain of music. From the moment of this first real talk, I have associated with our most terrible and earth-shaking critic a word which he often uses in his writing, though few remember it, when they, in turn, come to criticisms of him. It is "charm." Like a lost flower, charm is carried away on the flood of his invectives.

When these invectives began, I felt confronted not by the sword of the slayer but by a mighty tide—a literal flood-tide of speech rolling in, wave after wave, rising to a crest, subsiding, rising again, from the inexhaustible Great Lake of Mencken's absorbed and all-inclusive knowledge of what some might call (not he) the "folkways" of his country. The American scene, the American lot, the common American life, the faulty and factitious American democracy. I speak of a Great Lake, rather than of an ocean, for the waves were America-bound—except, perhaps, when he commended the fine tyrannical government of Frederick the Great—and they had, to my disaffected Puritan eye, used to the rocky northern seaboards, something a little featureless and uniform in their variety. Votes, senators, common decency, Bryan, Doctor Coolidge, boobs and yokels, button manufacturers, comstocks, wowsers, snouting and preposterous Puritans, "made for satirists as catnip was made for cats"—H. L. Mencken rolled them all on the beach—on his tongue—like so much wreckage, for my fascinated eyes.

"The German is Orson," says Meredith in his *Essay on Comedy,* a discriminating piece of analysis that the student of Mencken might profitably ponder, "or the mob, or a marching army, in defence of a good case or a bad—a big or a little. His irony is a missile of terrific tonnage; sarcasm he emits like a blast from a dragon's mouth. He must and will be Titan. He stamps his foe underfoot, and is astonished that the creature is not dead, but stinging; for in truth the Titan is contending, by comparison, with a god."

When Mencken speaks of New York, it is with one of these fiery serpent's blasts. But as he secretly knows, his adversary is a god. He is proud of his refusal to kneel at the altar of this great god, and maintains that in the metropolis he has only transitory friends. Has he ever taken the trouble to find out its quiet retreats and its permanent residents? Surely not. That would be unfaithfulness to Baltimore, and Mencken has an unbounded loyalty to the ties he accepts or inherits. He returns to New York for a hard bout

of work, and also for a raffish, Rabelaisian fling.
You should see the "bad-boy" expression that
comes over his face when he catalogues his knowledge of "speak-easies," and "good, old-fashioned
bars" back of the Jersey shore.

But suddenly—for I must return to the ciga-
rettes and the coffee and the cordial—a word was
spoken that had another echo than that of boot-
legger. It was LIBERTY. When that simple word
resounds about Mencken's head, the waves of
fluent speech recede. You see him, in the midst of
a silence, posing with rapt blue eyes for the picture of a revolutionist of '48, or of an adolescent
who has just won a contest with an autocratic
father. To use another image, it is as if the traffic
signals had changed, and a new light of faith had
come out in a doubter's face. This abstract good,
this liberty, is what my Algonquin host was in
need of. A fig for wine, women, and song! As
Diogenes searched for an honest man, so does the
editor of the *Mercury* search for a free Ameri-
cano. In drawing the portrait of William Jennings
Bryan at the Scopes trial, he also drew the self-
portrait of a lonely observer worth quoting in this
connection:

"When I first encountered him [Bryan] on the
side-walk in front of the office of the rustic lawyers who were his associates . . . the trial was
yet to begin, and he was still expansive and ami-

able. The old boy professed to be delighted with the argument, and gave the gaping bystanders to understand that I was a publicist of parts. Not to be outdone, I admired the preposterous country shirt that he wore—sleeveless and with the neck cut very low. We parted in the manner of two ambassadors. . . . The next day the battle joined. By the end of the week he was simply a walking fever. What the Christian Scientists call malicious animal magnetism seemed to radiate from him like heat from a stove. *From my place in the court room, standing upon a table, I looked directly down upon him, sweating horribly and pumping his palm-leaf fan. His eyes fascinated me; I watched them all day long. They were blazing points of hatred. They glittered like occult and sinister gems. Now and then they wandered to me, and I got my share, for my reports of the trial had come back to Dayton, and he had read them. It was like coming under fire.*"

It would have been worth a long journey to see the apostle of Liberty, standing on his table and staring down with curious, sea-blue eyes into the sinister orbs of the apostle of Fundamentalism. I believe that Mencken would sacrifice much for liberty, has indeed, with his strong courage, sacrificed much. Yet do not imagine that a trip to Dayton was a sacrifice. ". . . Here am I, a bachelor of easy means, forty-two years old, unham-

pered by debts or issues, able to go wherever I
please, and to stay as long as I please—here am I
contentedly and even snugly basking beneath the
Stars and Stripes." Staring at Bryan is one of
Mencken's ways of "basking." He would not ex-
change it for ten trips to Rome. "This eternal
struggle is sordid, but . . . it is also extremely
amusing. It brings out, as the moralists say, the
worst that is in human nature, *which is also the
most charming.*" The italics are mine, but mine is
not the "Catechism" that I quote from the end of
the Fifth Series of Prejudices:

"Q. If you find so much that is unworthy of
reverence in the United States, then why do you
live here?

"A. Why do men go to zoos?"

A JOURNALIST cited to me, apropos of the two
Menckens, the comedian of youth, whose tone
is not so different, except that it is mature, from
that of the *Harvard Lampoon* or any similar college paper, and the sardonic and solemn critic and
pamphleteer of our life and letters, who has made
himself a great national force, the story of the
man who went into a restaurant and first consumed a meal of sausage and *sauerkraut:* that was
for his tape worm. Then he ordered the meal of
an epicure: that was for himself. This solid and
sentimental family man of Baltimore, argued my

friend, the Mencken who believes in monogamy and proclaims that women should nurse their babies, and is sure that marriage is not a licensed week-end; this Puritanical sceptic, with his bookish and even scholarly tastes and his need of a familiar solitude in which to formulate in highly wrought phrases his scheme of fatalistic valuations —he is doubled by a discursive and immensely curious journalist, a man of broader ways and humours, who must keep in touch with the worst that is known and thought in his country, in order to ply the trade he entered upon as soon as he could escape from the family cigar-factory: the trade of destructive and ironic critic of his day and hour.

New York, even from Mencken's standpoint, is less pernicious than the hinterland of the rustic. But it is a place where the gifts that he esteems least—his gifts as a business man and a high-class journalist—can draw their provender. Stimulated and repletely amused, the comedian makes a jump for the Pennsylvania Station, and by the time he has reached Hollins Street, and entered into that solitary tomb of the serious writer which he has described so feelingly—the place where even Mencken has to fight with words and phrases to make them salient and responsive to his thought —he is again the civilized iconoclast, the almost tragic critic. "There was something," as he said of Beethoven, "Olympian in his rages, and there was a touch of hell fire in his mirth. . . . He concerns himself, not with the puerile agonies of love, but with the eternal tragedy of man. He is a great tragic poet, and like all great tragic poets, he is obsessed by a sense of the inscrutable meaninglessness of life. In his gorgeous music there went all of the high scepticism of the eighteenth century, but into it there also went the new enthusiasm, the new determination to challenge and beat the gods that dawned with the nineteenth century."

Mencken is not appraising himself when he thus appraises Beethoven. He is not appraising himself when he quotes Conrad as saying that his mission is "not to edify, to console, to improve or encourage but simply to get down on paper some shadow of his own eager sense of the wonder and prodigality of life as men lead it in this world, and of its unfathomable romance and mystery." But men shall be known by their admirations as well as by their hates, and Mencken's outspoken praise, his warm intuitive sympathies for these great fatalistic artists, is a kind of self-revelation. As from his championing of the Dreisers and the Willa Cathers and the Hergesheimers and the Cabells among native novelists, one can draw from such estimates a vision of the kind of American he is.

A non-Anglo-Saxon American, that is, a non-

Puritan, a man of European, rather than of British lineage. There is, as he says, undeniably "a difference in their primary instincts, in their reactions to common stimuli, in their ways of looking at the world, and that difference has, of late years, come to the estate of conflict, with the 'Anglo-Saxon' striving to keep what he has—his point of view, his cultural leadership, his political hegemony—and the non-'Anglo-Saxon' trying to take it away from him. . . . To admit the conflict is to admit his clear right, nay, his bounden duty to battle for his side, passionately, desperately, and with any weapon at hand."

I am thoroughly aware, when I spend two or three hours with Mencken, that he is the descendant of gregarious, agnostic, scholarly, musical, extraverted Germans, saturated for centuries in the common life of the café, and the market-place, and the popular classical concert, while I descend from lonely New England farmers and doctors and divines who meditated on eternity and morality and the state of their souls as they pursued their introverted and difficult lives. Mencken, though so much of a romantic Nietzschean individualist, hates and loathes his solitude as a writer, rages against it as he rages about his amenities, and worries not at all about his soul. Theoretically he loves to stand alone, a superior individual whose mission it is to resist and survive. Practically and actually he is a very gregarious human who enjoys a drummer or a Babbitt much better than a cultured man, studies his customs and his ideas and even his speech with close attention—consider that remarkable scholarly work, *The American Language*—though he cannot endure being governed by his opinions.

The New Englanders I descend from were all theoretical democrats, believers in town meetings and group action. Actually and practically they were non-gregarious, non-satirical, moralistic or altruistic, aristocratic in their tastes, and had little or no use or gift for the mixed contacts of the market-place. These are indeed "real differences." Speaking as a dissident from the race that is being superseded, as one who has assimilated certain aspects of European culture and learned with some difficulty that there is humour as well pathos and innocent goodness in Babbittry, I can agree with Edmund Wilson that Mencken represents "the civilized consciousness of modern America, its learning, its intelligence, and its tastes, realizing the grossness of the American manners and mind, and crying out in horror and chagrin."

Henry Louis Mencken was born in the year 1880 in Baltimore. His life may already be found, *in extenso,*—such is our biographical age—in the compendious volume of Isaac Goldberg, Ph.D. If

Mencken ever laughs at himself (I am not sure), it must have been when he saw those despised professorial stigmata on the cover. He himself, being an exceedingly personal writer—"What is in the head infallibly oozes out through the nub of the pen"—has told us practically everything we want to know about the mature Mencken, even to possibly undesired details of manicuring and pyjamas. That he does so, rather consciously and objectively and, when the comedian's manner is upon him, brazenly, I gather from sentences like this: "An author, like any other so-called artist, is a man to whom the normal vanity of all men is so vastly exaggerated that he finds it a sheer impossibility to hold it in. His overpowering impulse is to gyrate before his fellow men, flapping his wings and emitting defiant yells. This being forbidden by the Polizei of all civilized countries, he takes it out by putting his yells on paper. Such is the thing called self-expression." Mencken does laugh at himself, sardonically enough. I wonder whether the editors of the *Yale Review*, the *New Republic*, the *Saturday Review of Literature*, or even the *New Yorker* would relish themselves as this Mercurial editor does in the guise of strutting fowls.

It is from Goldberg, rather than from Mencken, however, that I have learned his family history. His grandfather Mencken came to Baltimore in 1848 (not, we are assured, as a revolutionary patriot) entered a tobacco factory—for the German Menckens, earlier of the professional classes, had become men of commerce—bought a general store, founded a tobacco factory of his own, a solid business which was continued by Mencken's father. The grandfather, in the childhood of young Henry, was a domineering old patriarch in a long-tailed black coat and "archaic" collars, who dosed his twenty grandchildren and drove them out in his swarming buggy. The father, another hard-headed, autocratic business man, destined his eldest son, Henry, for the tobacco business. Mencken often tells us that he inherited his agnostic habit of mind, as well as his liking for practical joking, from his male ancestors. He would not, perhaps, allow as easily that inversely he may have drawn from this same dominant source his strong dislike for business as a profession, and his male view—clear in the general and particular tone of his works— that women are very secondary to the constructive lives of men.

Henry had intentions of his own about his career. Having read *Huckleberry Finn* when he was six, beginning "seriously" to write by his twelfth year—he has characteristically preserved his first very creditable work, on "A New Platinum Toning Bath for Silver Prints"—having been, *mirabile dictu,* confirmed at the age of fifteen in the

Lutheran Church, having turned to poetic and musical composition, while at the Baltimore Polytechnic, having adopted Huxley as his god, he determined to become a journalist. His time in the factory was brief. His father died, he took over the headship of the family, and once and for all settled down to live with his mother, and got an assignment on the Baltimore *Morning Herald*.

By 1903 he was city editor. By 1905, at the age of twenty-five, he was editor-in-chief. The next year he moved to the more famous *Sun*, where he stayed until 1917. His most notable work there was done for his free-lance column—the birthplace of the "Maryland Free State," of which he is so justly proud. He became literary critic of the *Smart Set* in 1908, to Nathan's dramatic critic; and thus began his long and affectionate association with the new literature and the new authors, like Dreiser, whom he helped so materially to show their heads above the walls of Puritan prejudice. Editor of the magazine in 1914, then owner, with Nathan, and finally editor of the *American Mercury*: this is the bare outline.

ADD to this dry chronicle a vast number of "allied activities" in the field of critical letters, including the publication of many books, and you have a career, multifariously active, agressively successful, robust, and exuberant; one of the most significant in modern America. Here is a vigorous, trained mind, with sensitive literary and artistic perceptions and strong scientific interest, propelled by a temperament at once ruthless, fearless, and militant. Mencken disclaims idealism, scholarship, evangelism; yet he is really a sort of sadistic evangelist, a Puritan with a scalpel instead of a Bible, who is all the people he condemns. "It is difficult," he admits, "for an American to contemplate an American without something comparable to moral indignation." Mencken's indignation and his isolation grow with the years. When he had gathered about himself a fairly numerous group of creative literary spirits—about his earlier self, the critic as artist, who smashed the old idols of wholesomeness and respectability—he turned away from them. They no longer needed him. Their cause was won. The parlous state of the democratic state called him to new and more bitter social action. The *American Mercury* takes less interest in the arts than the *Smart Set* of old, and more in social phenomena. The partnership with Nathan, which belonged to the æsthetic years, was here dissolved, and one finds the social critics, the historians, the doctors and scientists, taking the floor. Mencken admits that he can scarcely now read a current novel. "He will be mayor of Baltimore in five years," remarked Nathan sagely.

Just then Mencken stuck his head with its goblin ears through the door to summon his delicate friend to lunch. "I hear you are to be mayor of Baltimore?"—"No, I refused the office. But I may run for senator."

Take it as a joke or a prophecy, but be assured that *Notes on Democracy*, that fierce, surgical diagnostic and dissection of our democratic scheme—"I am not engaged in therapeutics but in pathology"—is regarded by the author as his most important work. It is based on the theory that men are not alike, that politics is not soluble by the seraphic intuition of the boobs, "that the world is a vast field of greased poles flying gaudy and seductive flags. Up each a human soul goes shinning, painfully and with many a slip. Some climb eventually to high levels; a few scale the dizziest heights. But the great majority never get very far from the ground. There they struggle for a while and then give it up. The effort is too much for them: it doesn't seem to be worth its agonies. Golf is easier; so is joining Rotary; so is Fundamentalism; so is osteopathy; so is Americanism." Democracy is the government of the envious, of those who cannot allow their superiors—the ideally educated modern men, who have put away the immemorial fears of the race and are sure of themselves in this world—a chance to rule them. Democratic man hates the fellow who is having a better time than he, as the Puritan and the Prohibitionist do.

Is Mencken going by his invectives to swell the company of the governing aristocrats, as he undoubtedly swelled the company of the free writers? Is he by his words of scorn bringing out of their holes men of "common decency," who do not buy votes or office—or compromise with ideas or jobs? He seems to doubt it.

"The free man is one who has won a small and precarious territory from the great mob of his inferiors, and is prepared and ready to defend it and make it support him. All around him are enemies, and where he stands there is no friend. He can hope for little help from other men of his own kind, for they have battles of their own to fight. He has made himself a sort of god in his little world, and he must face the responsibilities of a god, and the dreadful loneliness." That passage, as much as any in Swift's great satires, seems to spring from a tragic source.

Mencken, it is well known, is a dominating contemporary influence in our universities. Yet he is not, in any daily human sense, close to the young. He still stands on a table of isolation, above these young collegians who stretch out their hands to him. Life, says Horace Walpole, is a comedy to those who think, a tragedy to those who feel.

It is easy to see whence the legend of Mencken the slayer arose. Straight from the books. Looking toward the human being, I see a man with bright blue eyes and a gentle mouth, listening to a strain of music, and surrounded by old and even elderly friends—mostly doctors and musicians and journalists, the happiest companions Baltimore has to offer. Mencken's friends know him as a man of originality, "hence of genuine charm." A man with a wine cellar. A man extraordinarily free. A man who has had a rare time, in that silent study which is his tomb and his solace, in charging innocent words with his own powerful brand of dynamite, and arranging them in his own dangerous pattern. They know him as a man who likes to do a good turn to the very under dogs he affects to despise, and who would ill endure, himself, the iron rule of a tyrant or a Mussolini. They know him as a romantic adventurer in the field of sex, who feels love to be the business of the cool of the evening, when a man's work is done. They know him as one who has furnished more ideas to other men than any living American critic. Perhaps Mencken has failed to live up to the tradition of his substantial, patriotic tribe, good citizens of the Free State, by remaining a bachelor. But the descendants of an original and generous artist are not always children of flesh and blood. They are sometimes, like Mr. Babbitt—Mr. Boob—the children of other men's brains.

# CHAPTER XIII
# WILLA CATHER
*Prairie Cliff*

WILLA CATHER

*Camera Portrait by E. O. Hoppé*

# WILLA CATHER

*Prairie Cliff*

ILLA CATHER has arrived very quietly at her high place in American letters. Her life, her work, and her personality have a simple unity and consistency that are frequently found in literary personalities in Europe but rarely in our own country, though she is the very sort of American whom Londoners would enjoy as "characteristic"—a woman with a western flavour in her speech and bearing that twenty years or so of residence on Manhattan Island have not rendered less invigorating. An editorial interview with her at *McClure's Magazine* in the old days—when her dreams as a writer were still unfulfilled—was like a draught of champagne. One felt life and impatience with life brimming and foaming in her, and went away roused and teased oneself by the sudden swirl and prick of bubbles rising from the depths. She lived then in Washington Square, she still lives near by, and likes to pace the paths below the statue of Garibaldi; if one hails her there on a happy spring afternoon, in her familiar clothes of some fresh brown or green—which challenge a little, as her spirit does, the blandishments of the passing age—her face in its fine maturity shines out with the selfsame frankness of her youth, the same warmth and resolute strength of prairie wind and sun. Unless, of course, she has just happened upon some especially offensive gift of the year—such as a paragraph in the gossip column of the press. Then her countenance contracts to closed and negative lines, and her whole person turns aloof and prickly with scorn and rejection.

If all our fiction writers had brought with them to the metropolis this power of rejection we should have had more fine American novels and fewer cheap successes. How Willa Cather hates cheapness! She may not have had a richer creative endowment than many others. But she had more certainty of aim. More power of self-protection. More insight into the ultimate fruits of easy opportunity and popularity. More character, if one is to speak truly—and if character means certain old-fashioned virtues like faith, grit, determination, and unremitting labour. One of the things that a young New Englander recognized most clearly in her long ago was a standard: a standard of living, which made of a modest existence and simple tastes something comely and satisfying; a standard of literary excellence which was based on deep love and knowledge of the "masters." She knew as clearly as a child the proper food of her spirit—Wagnerian opera, for instance, the stories of Mérimée and Turgeniev, walks in Central Park, French wine and French cooking, the society of musical artists and old friends from Pittsburgh and the West. She was vigorous and single-minded and thoroughly unaccomodating in temper. I think of her as having, then and now, the clear-cut, resistant, woman nature that is associated with primitives. Adaptability, either feminine or urbane, was not in her. The greater part of the people, the ideas, the aims, the social amusements that crossed her path were alien to her, and she made no bones of refusing them as unassimilable and unimportant. She must have been about thirty years old when I first met her, and her objective hung as clear as a new moon above the electric glitter of New York. She would have scorned to create her reputation until she had really earned it. She had accepted as final the hypothesis—or is it the fact?—that a complete and loyal devotion to an art means a definite sacrifice of life. "Happiness"—so she has put it in a story, commenting on Tolstoy's credo—"lies in ceasing to be and to cause being, because the thing revealed to us is dearer than any existence our appetites can ever get for us." A pioneer upbringing may be as fine an armour for art as it is for breaking the glebe, and Willa Cather, by those prairie roots of hers, seems to belong to a more steadfast, as to a more reticent, generation than that of her literary contemporaries.

Her eastern existence has always had a western counterpart as essential to her as the soul to the body. Red Cloud, Nebraska, and its hinterland, which in the days of her childhood would have been considered a highly inauspicious place for a writer to grow up in, continues to know and cherish her as its leading citizen. Well it may, since the formative history of the state has been written down more literally as well as more lyrically in her pages than it ever will be in more strictly historical works—or in the stories of a later brood of mid-western novelists, more interested than she in surfaces. Now that her portrait by Bakst hangs in Omaha, now that *My Ántonia* is translated into French and into Czech, and all the books have been translated into the Swedish language, it is natural that young students all over the corn belt should decide to grow to fame by writing up the farm neighbours. Yet how many of these hard-headed young realists will know how to contribute as she has done—with only Virgil as an early guide —to the sum total of happiness on lonely ranches?

How many of them shall receive, when they move on to New York, culinary offerings addressed to the "best book writer in the world"? It was related in Hastings that a certain old Bohemian farmer, who had been brought into the hospital, and who wished to recommend himself to his doctor's good graces, introduced himself thus modestly: "I am the husband of My Ántonia." The story dovetails very neatly with a paragraph towards the end of this same novel where the boy Jim Burden, studying his lessons in the lamplight, broods over his professor's explanation of a passage in the Georgics. *Primus ego in patriam meam—deducam Musas. I was the first to bring the Muse into my country.* "This was not a boast but a hope, at once bold and devoutly humble, that he might bring the Muse not to the capital but to his father's fields, sloping down to the river and to the old beech-trees with broken tops."

A hope, a wish, they are one and the same when held with intensity. As Mr. Forrester, the husband of the Lost Lady, once put it to his guests, it is the secret wish of the heart that turns great dreams—those of railroad builders, those of novelists—into constructive realities. Like most of the boys in Willa Cather's stories, Jim Burden, through whose eyes the story of Ántonia is remembered, is in some sort an incarnation of the author. Reading it, I visualize as observer not a boy but a tomboy: a

girl with a charming open face, obstinate blue
eyes, and shingled red-brown hair; a girl who drew
deep into her lungs the wild, free breath of the
land to which she had been transplanted from
Virginia, and in the grandiose human outline of
its pioneer settlers from old Europe, standing
against the broad fields and wide sky, beheld the
figures of her destiny. There is something primordial in Willa Cather's voice, her eyes, her gestures, when she speaks of these figures to-day.
It is clear that a few obscure lives—Bohemian,
Swedish, French—have contributed as profoundly
to the strength of her affections as the richness
and glory of the untamed prairie, and its slow
transformation into corn and wheat have contributed to her robustness as an artist. In the days
when a wild little girl rode her pony twelve miles
over the rough red grass of the Divide to fetch the
mail—the letters and newspapers of the immi-
grant neighbours too, with their queer foreign
words and strange coloured inks, which irritated
her by their inscrutability—the unwritten history
of the country was beginning in her heart, as she
has recorded that it began in that of Alexandra,
the pioneer woman. And from the hour, many
years later, when she was able to renounce her
editorship for the career of literature, it seems that
her most illumined hours have been spent, not in
scrutinizing or absorbing the present, as many

266

writers do, but in looking backward with intensity to her "father's fields," as an Indian remembers the beauties of his legendary world. It is not accidental that O Pioneers! and My Ántonia and A Lost Lady have something of the force of myth or epic. "Mental excitement was apt to send me back with a rush to my own naked land and the figures scattered upon it. They accompanied me through all my new experiences."

T HE books, taken not too literally, are symbolic of the several stages of this fine life, which began so decorously in the crystallized, old-fashioned south, burst into flower in the wild west, and then compressed itself gradually into the sophisticated pattern of the eastern seaboard. I am waiting for the novel that will reveal the story of the early Virginia years that Willa Cather remembers vividly and sometimes recalls aloud—as, for example her revolt from polite feudal traditions, from "layers and layers of life," too neatly stratified, from the benevolent judge who, patting the curls of a sweet little girl, was received with the fury of two clenched fists and the cry—one that all friends of this prickly soul will relish: "I'se a dang'ous nigger, I is!" Willa Cather is still a "dang'ous nigger" to those who violate her privacies, or seek to make her a vulgar celebrity.

The journey to Nebraska at the age of eight

left its mark. The novelist remembers the look of the Great Lakes, her sorrow at leaving them behind. The family was bound for the ranch of her grandfather and she remembers, too, what it felt like to be shut up in the house at first with elder relatives—what it was like to escape at last, on a windy March day, into the spacious, untouched glory of the Divide. We may think of O *Pioneers!* her first really achieved long story, as picturing rather closely the conditions which prevailed at the period of her arrival at her grandmother's, when the turf dwellings of the first settlers were being replaced by frame houses and only great wills could dominate the wilderness, and great visions confront an uncertain future. *My Ántonia* begins also on the Divide at a still more drastic era, which she knew from her elders' stories, some fifteen years earlier than O *Pioneers!* in historical time, and continues into a later day when Red Cloud (Black Hawk), the pioneer town, and the lower road by the creek and the cottonwoods superseded the Divide in the girl's daily experience. The earlier part of *The Song of the Lark* adds also to the picture, especially the chapters where figures the beloved Dr. Archie. For Dr. Archie understood a girl who had to go her own way and needed the Latin of a priest rather than the lessons of the district school. Take the three books together and you will find, like brilliant threads in a tapestry, the most radiant of Willa Cather's early memories, intuitions, and impressions of the Nebraska *patria*.

In *A Lost Lady* one feels a greater modification of memory by mature experience. It relates a literal human history of the Red Cloud region, in the days when the railroad-building aristocracy lived along the Burlington. But while the image of Mrs. Forrester is enshrined by mellow visual impressions of sandy creeks and wide meadows and poplars which the story-teller must have salted away these many years in the tears of youth, the romantic and disconcerting "Lady" herself stands before us in the light of a sophisticated knowledge which no young memory has in its stores. As for *One of Ours,* a book that the author herself ranks, for its stark outlines, above her other works, that brings the Nebraska farmer up to date—at least up to the dull, rich period before the war, when machinery had replaced hand labour, and sharp business methods the hardy faith of the pioneer. This, to her, decadent epoch, Willa Cather knew as a returned and sentimental pilgrim, rather than as a native daughter, and it may be that one reason why she so respects the artistic verities of her novel is that they wounded her so sorely as she set them down. She is enough of a Puritan idealist to take fidelity to disillusion as a sort of penance. The Great War—which one thinks of as the only "world event" that has deeply affected her—enabled her to make up to her "rough-neck" hero for the sterility of the present mid-western farmer's destiny. One of the most endearing things about this vivid and distinguished writer is a suspicion, humbly harboured, that she herself is a rough-neck in disguise who has only happened into fame. I feel in her sympathy for Claude a generous desire to help the others to their great adventure. But here her Muse betrayed her a little. For when Claude's adventure took him to France, it dimmed before our eyes. The prairie farm was the centre where the War affected Willa Cather, and the image of Claude and his mother clinging together "in the pale square of the west window, as the two natures in one person meet and cling in a fated hour" is the one that will survive. For this woman has to touch life at first hand, in order to create it.

*The Song of the Lark* falls, in point of chronology, between *O Pioneers!* and *My Ántonia*, carries over from the western childhood to the period of inevitable artistic and youthful revolt— "artist's youth"—which whirled Willa Cather out into the great world, as it did her heroine, to seek gifts and advantages that Nebraska could not give. The mature artist in Willa Cather repudiates much of this book, would like to reduce it by at least a third. The theme is the evolution of a woman not unlike a certain great Wagnerian singer and the latter is said to have exclaimed to the author, on reading it: "I don't know where you begin and I end!" It breathes a robust life and passionate longing for self-expression to which young western women of strong professional ambition still respond. I saw such a one from the Pacific coast who had made her way to the seats of the mighty and could have kissed the ground Willa Cather walked on.

The girl herself, the future novelist, who never dreamed of becoming Willa Cather, though she did dream of a great vocation, graduated from the university where she had supported herself by newspaper work at the age of nineteen, and having immediately found a job as dramatic reporter on a Pittsburgh paper, plunged eastward to cultivated joys like music, and human relations of which she had heretofore been starved. Her single volume of poetry, *April Twilights*, dates from this time. The best of the very promising short stories which she began to write, such as "The Sculptor's Funeral" and "Paul's Case"—and these best are as fine as anything she has done since— do not derive their motive force from the radiation of memory, but from the bitterness of revolt from limitations. Originally published in a volume called *The Troll Garden*, long since out of print, they were again made accessible in the collection of short stories called *Youth and the Bright Medusa,* most of which were written at a later period. The book, wholly concerned with art and artists—Willa Cather's passion for artists, especially musical artists, has been second only to her passion for pioneers—may be taken as a sort of commentary on the contacts of the full and ardent Pittsburgh years, supplemented by those of New York. The singers who came through Pittsburgh to get the dollars of the iron kings would tell things to an eager young reporter because she cared so *terribly* to hear. (It may be we have a faint image of this young Cather in the earnest girl who beset and comforted Oswald with her companionship and her desire for knowledge, when Myra was wrestling with her mortal enemy.) If you want to know how New York looked to a young woman of twenty-eight, spurred by an artistic ambition, read that glorious short story, "Coming, Aphrodite!" which has in it the old, the real Washington Square, and the passing love-affair of a painter and a singer. The artists of the Metropolitan and the great music masters welcomed as one of themselves a woman writer who fully understood their medium. Looking back to this time, when Willa Cather was writing *The Song of the Lark,* it seems to me that as we walked around the Reservoir in Central Park, the very sunsets over the snow and the city faded away to an opera air; as just after the war the tender spring grass was red with the blood of soldier boys. I have never known anyone so wholly centred in an imaginative work. All terrestrial subjects, all metropolitan life, that do not contribute to it might be lunar while it is under way, so far as the obsessed author is concerned.

W HEN Willa Cather came to New York from Pittsburgh it was to join the staff of *McClure's Magazine*. But the magazine under the stimulating direction of S. S. McClure, at the height of the muck-raking era, offered no real oasis to the writer of novels. Yet the editor managed to produce a number of short stories and a short novel, called *Alexander's Bridge*. The latter represented in theme and technique more of a concession to popular standards than she ever permitted herself again. Willa Cather was devoted to her "Chief," but she had as much resistance to muck-raking and social reform then as she has to the psychology of Freud to-day, perhaps for the same reason. The spirit of the age, as I have suggested, does not greatly affect her at any time, and she fought the implications of the magazine world, all the six years of her stay in it. The one great happiness that she found in a magazine assignment came to her in Boston, because her sojourn there brought about a friendship with Sarah Orne

Jewett that proved one of the richest of her life. The letters to Willa Cather in the published letters of the New England author reveal her sense of the promise of the fresh young Westerner, and suggest the degree to which a creative mind which has schooled itself to canons of honesty and perfection may be yeast and wine to another in a more malleable stage. I can imagine the author of *A Lost Lady* writing just such a letter as this of Sarah Jewett's, of December 1908, to a girl she took an interest in:

My Dear Willa:

I cannot help saying what I think about your writing and its being hindered by such incessant, important, responsible work as you have in your hands now. . . . If you don't keep and guard and mature your force, and above all have time and quiet to perfect your work, you will be writing things not much better than you did five years ago. . . . You must find a quiet place near the best companions (not those who admire and wonder at everything one does, but those who know the good things with delight!) . . . Otherwise what might be strength in a writer is only crudeness, and what might be insight is only observation; sentiment falls to sentimentality—you can write about life, but never write life itself. And to write and work on this level, we must live on it—we must at least recognize it and defer to it at every step. . . . To work in silence and with all one's heart, that is the writer's lot; he is the only artist who must be solitary, and yet needs the widest outlook upon the world.

T HE most complete expression of Willa Cather's own artistic creed is to be found in the admirable preface to a selection of Sarah Orne Jewett's work that she has recently edited: "The artist spends his life loving things that haunt him, in having his mind teased by them, in trying to get them down on paper exactly as they are to him." And to achieve anything noble, anything enduring, he must give himself absolutely to his material. The gift of sympathy is his greatest gift, the fine thing which alone can make his work fine. "He fades away into the land and people of his heart, he dies of love only to be born again." So Sarah Jewett died in *The Country of the Pointed Firs*, so Willa Cather died a prairie death in *O Pioneers!* and again, a greater, in *My Antonia, A Lost Lady*, in the first half of *One of Ours*.

W ILLA CATHER herself says that the moment when she stopped trying to *write*—that is, to write according to an invented formula—and began to *remember* was the one when her literary vocation claimed its rights. It was then that the finer novels began to emerge from the matrix of her mind with the west as their most inevitable scene. *O Pioneers!* is not a fabricated thing, but a true recreation of experience, and the act of writing from that day forth became, not a pain, a struggle, an imprisonment, as it is to many, but literally a *recreation*, a holiday. "It is what poker is to my brother." Another of her phrases gives a clue: "It is a complete loss of self for three hours a day." Perhaps *My Mortal Enemy* suggests what a woman of a "dangerous," rebellious heart might feel if she had no outlet, no other preoccupation for her energies and gifts than a shabby and ineffectual husband.

On the feeling side it seems that Willa Cather's satisfaction flows from the fact that her books are always transcriptions of friendships for people or places. Though she has distilled the warm and loyal admiration of her nature into the cool stream of art, her relation to her central character or country has remained intense and deeply affectionate. And there is always a central personage in the books, like a priceless *objet d'art* on a drawing-room table, whose interest and beauty are supreme. Willa Cather's great aim as a storyteller has been, as she once explained to a group of English teachers, to get "across" to her readers something direct about this beloved object— as a boy would succeed in conveying to a sister just arrived from Europe his feeling about the girl he was engaged to marry. Sometimes she does this through description, sometimes merely through characteristic speech, sometimes through incident. In any case character is conveyed by suggestion rather than by analysis, and reveals itself usually not as God's objective observation of a human creature, but as the ardent notation of a secondary devoted personage.

On the intellectual side her fun has largely been in experiments in form. Colour of a florid sort is more native to her talent than line, and her progress as an artist, to her own thinking, has come about by making colour mean form. This has been her hardest task. She has sought, in Robert Frost's phrase, the purification of her quality, and has accepted as her quality a certain sparseness and austerity in line and contour. Where she has tried for fullness of life, as in *The Song of the Lark,* she has failed in large measure. "Tom Outland's Story" is the most strikingly coloured part of *The Professor's House,* but far less moving than those last serene thirty pages where the Professor distils his life's memories. Yet the author does believe in allowing herself considerable latitude in the general shape of a novel. She conceives that the form it has assumed for her mind's eye at the fiery second of its explosion in her consciousness is the inevitable one. There is always such an explosion for a novel, as for a poem, and the more closely the shape it tears is adhered to, the less it is tinkered with, the better the result.

Life for her, so far as her earlier books record it, falls into two great patterns: the pioneer or

277

farm pattern, with its immutable relations, father and daughter, sister and brother, mother and son, grandmother and grandchild, and its dumb, struggling ideals; the artist pattern, with its sparkling, superhuman aims and ambitions, and its imperfect and fragile human ties. Through both patterns breaks, now and then, a great wave of overwhelming emotion from below the crust of things; that is her only interest in the "subconscious," with which so many of her generation are concerned. As for the crust—the visual, tangible, natural world, though so dear to her, she knows to be only valuable to her characters where they touch, smell, look at it. The hot, fecund prairie, the arid cliff up-standing in blue, south-western air, live in her books because human beings behold and covet them. There Willa Cather is glad to be with the "elders," as she says, rather than with the Imagists and the reportorial school.

Love, to the central character—always a woman up to now, save in the case of Claude and the Professor, for Willa Cather is likely to see women as the more romantic element in any novel, especially in novels of the pioneer west, and often sees them through the eyes of a subordinate male—is usually incidental to a larger career: usually illicit, usually devastating, or only happy for one poignant and lyrical moment. Remember, for instance, the tragic interlude of Marie and Emil, in *O Pioneers!* The author does not believe in domestic bliss. Indeed it is only with *A Lost Lady* and the books that have followed that she has attacked the normal domestic life of the sophisticated, and she does it with a kind of aversion, a kind of reluctance, that seems a part of the greater compression, the greater austerity of background that is manifest in her later work. In *A Lost Lady* the poetry of memory, together with the stringency of the compression, produced her masterpiece, a beautiful novel that has been called the finest published in any country since the war; a novel whose disillusions are full of illusion. But I think I shall always love better the early books which comprehend youth and simplicity so largely and profoundly than the later ones where the ugliness, the complexity of middle or old age pierce through. It is as if this "modern life" from which Willa Cather had tried to protect her writing had "got in at" her after all. She does not want to probe its depths, and its surfaces wound her. Even the Professor, whom she understands so intuitively, must point the truth that the day we live in is ugly and claptrap; that what one reaches for in the feeling relations of life is likely to betray. That only what one puts into it by way of personal creative effort abides.

THERE is a river in the Wind River Mountains in Wyoming—one of her happy hunting-grounds —that after leaping torrentially down the side of a mountain vanishes, with all its glittering waters, into the dark base of the mountain itself. But a mile further down the mountain in a deep, still pool green with marsh grass, another river starts, a gentle, smooth-flowing, level stream. These two are one and the same. So Willa Cather conceives the artist's life as it should be; so, when one visits her in her book-lined rooms in Bank Street, one feels that it is. About the rooms are evidences of the more torrential course: paintings of Italy and the south-west; relics of Sarah Orne Jewett's Maine coast, autographed photographs of famous singers and writers of European fame; lithographs of Czechoslovakia. Courbet's Georges Sand is over the mantel, and Keats—a Boston literary heirloom—is in the background. I know that I shall find there on a winter's day a coal grate fire, as if it were England. There will be yellow daffodils, if the spring is near enough, there will be hot buttery crumpets for tea, passed perhaps by a niece from Nebraska; there will be new books; and if I stay for dinner, and lay my things on her grandmother's patchwork quilt, I shall look forward to a perfect salad-dressing made by the hostess, and a mellow winebottle. But there are no obvious signs of greater celebrity about the apartment than there were years ago, and Willa Cather will, as always, tell me how noisy the neighbours are and that the only thing popularity has done for her is to take from her the one thing she values: time. But for this matter she remains thrifty and resourceful, and her novels come along as certainly nowadays as the elections and the seasons.

The author's skin is warm and ruddy, her eyes are sailor blue, her bluff, almost boyish address is modified by a little catch at the beginning of a sentence that might be shyness or just eager zest of life restrained by thought—as the river is caught in the weight of the mountain. And if she talks, as she may of her friend Ántonia, with her fourteen children, who doesn't want to die because she would have to stop cooking, I feel again what it has meant to my friend to grow up in a land that was "not a country at all but the material out of which countries are made." A country "with motion in it." A country where she learned so young the happiness it is "to be dissolved into something complete and great." A country that inspired her most poetic vein. That fine legendary narrative of the south-west, *Death Comes to the Archbishop,* has something of the clear, flowing movement of *Robinson Crusoe.*

Once when Willa Cather and I walked on the

rocky shore of Massachusetts in winter she told me with a mixture of amusement and annoyance how her young sister whom she was then sending to an eastern college had complained, when she showed her Gloucester Harbour, that she could not see the sunset because there were "too many masts." I think the novelist feels the large, bold essentials and simplicities to be thus obscured in New York. Perhaps she has spent more years in Bank Street than in Red Cloud, more hours in Carnegie Hall than on the rock of Acoma. Yet on the windswept Divide she stands, on the red resistant rock, untamed, insurgent, ungiving, save to the writing that fulfils her, the past that claims her, the generous youth and the loyal friends whom she fiercely and almost blindly cherishes.

# CHAPTER XIV

# ROBERT FROST

*Good Greek out of New England*

ROBERT FROST

*Camera Portrait by E. O. Hoppé*

## ROBERT FROST

*Good Greek out of New England*

OBERT FROST'S spirit is native to all high, sweet-smelling, lonely slopes which command, as from a remove, the homes and the graves of men. Of such places he has seemed to me, ever since I first read *A Boy's Will,* the *genius loci.* If I watched long enough he might put off his trick of invisibility and show his head above a blueberry bush or a boulder. No doubt I have searched for him most persistently in the pastures below the ledgy shoulder of Chocorua, but I once thought I spied him in a sunburned cliff city of New Mexico, and his elusive figure is associated with the high glare of Delphi, and with those jagged little peaks of southern France whence the scent of herbs rises like incense. Those who mistake his verse for a product local or provincial have been too literal. They have failed to catch the poet in his game of hide-and-seek. Frost does hide, if he can, in verse or out. The language of his poetry, though so markedly that of New England speech, is symbolic; his subject-matter, for all its clear geographical limits, is universal. Through the realism of the lines, stars and "charted meteors" are always piercing. Like his friend the Star-splitter, Frost seems once for all to have burned down his house for the insurance, and spent the proceeds on a telescope,

> To satisfy a life-long curiosity
> About our place among the infinities.

He has been interrogating the heavens ever since. That may be the reason why he is still, as he puts it in "New Hampshire"—the most openly autobiographical of his poems—"a rascal," instead of the learned doctor or the celebrated bard he might be if he chose.

A kind of professor he has had to be in spite of himself, since most good Greeks—Frost almost admits himself one in "New Hampshire," as well as a plain farmer—from Socrates on have needed to add youth to their star-gazing. Frost affirms that he has "never earned a cent, save from and through verse. But for my first twenty years at it I earned a total of two hundred dollars." Farming and teaching, those two subsidiary occupations with which he has had almost as lifelong a connection as with the infinities, grew somehow out of his poems, as poems so surely grew out of them. In the early days it was more farming than teaching. Latterly it has been the other way about. Frost is too suspicious of formal learning to have become a pedagogue easily. It was not, so he tells, until he found the store-keeper at Derry, New Hampshire—where by the grace of a grandfather with no faith in the Muses he had that first farm of his—appraising his horse for the grocery bill that he decided to apply (with a poem) at Pinkerton Academy. He would prove to the world of men that he could have as much practical success as he wanted. But there was more for Frost in teaching than a solution of household economics, or we should not find him still trailing, in the Amherst hills or the Michigan flats, his troop of college boys.

Even when he consents to sit on a platform he has a vanishing and peripatetic look, and the doctrine he enunciates in his dry, sly, halting way is very different from the glib æstheticism his students might expect of a poet. Perfectionist and polisher of words though he is, he proclaims words to be "less than nothing unless they amount to deeds, as in ultimatums and battle cries." In poetry, as in life, there is no worth in being unless it is allied to doing. And what kind of professor is this who gives you no synthetic appreciations, and forces you to speculate? The day I saw him on an Amherst platform he was steering his class towards the reading of Emerson by asking it to define an "idealist." Is he a man who measures up from nothing, or one who measures down from everything? Might he be, especially if an artist, somewhere between the two? "I believe in what the Greeks called synecdoche: the philosophy of the part for the whole; skirting the hem of the goddess. All that an artist needs is samples. Enough success to know what money is like; enough love to know what women are like." Enough time, he might have added, for creative puttering; enough thin books of verse to fill half a foot of shelf. Frost is always bedevilling his students with questions, but never with one—this is his cardinal principle as an educator—which he can answer himself. For example this poser: How many things can you do to a poem besides read it or write it? The class found one hundred and eight. Compare the passage in "A Fountain":

> How had the tender verse escaped their outrage?
> By being invisible for what it was,
> Or else by some remoteness that defied them
> To find out what to do to hurt a poem.

One of the outstanding facts about Robert Frost is that he and his verse were buried for twenty years in the rocky quietude of New Hampshire. It is not so sure that even now college students—

or for that matter college teachers, publishers, editors, critics, and friendly readers—know what to make of the cast of mind and spirit of a good Greek disguised as a Yankee sage.

The cast of feature bears out the cast of mind. If I could choose a sculptor from the antique world to mould Frost's head, I should vote for Skopas, who added shadows of human passion to calm Greek faces. In certain moods, this Frost face with its musing eyes, so deeply hollowed and shaded by sharp-drawn brows, seems touched by that pathetic hand. But again the poet's dream grows unified, grave, mystical-religious, and one says, here are a brow and eyes like Dante's. At the dinner in honour of Frost's fiftieth birthday at the Hotel Brevoort, in New York, he wore at first this marble Dantesque mask; coloured really like Carrara marble, with mauve and golden shadows, and shining with a clear Renaissance beauty of the Christian sort. Frost should have wrapped himself in a white Domonican gown to celebrate his half century. For he carried almost visibly the consecration and weight of his ascetic priesthood.

Yet it took only a featherweight of affection— all that the friends dared offer, since they had come, for the most part, with the hands that bore gifts tied behind their backs—to make tenderness flicker like flame over the still features, and shape itself in facial line; only a quip of New England humour to bring a gentle cynic out of hiding. Or shall I say a rustic deity? Eyebrows arch roundly, cheeks draw into shrewd, satiric wrinkles, eyes turn to flashes and darts of blue light, malicious or rejoicing, and as an unruly lock is tossed, one hears the stamp of a hoof—

> Pan came out of the woods one day.
> His skin and his hair and his eyes were grey . . .

Frost's skin and his rebellious hair have now a fine harmony of tone, "the grey of the moss of walls," a young and living greyness that, like a delicate lichen, softens without hiding the hard and eternal shape of the rock beneath.

> —a new-world song, far out of reach.

that is what the rascally Pan of the haunting Yankee pipe came out of the woods to play. Poetry has not flowed in a swelling stream from the pipe of Robert Frost; it has been distilled within him preciously, like heart's-blood, drop by drop. The verse reveals a keen warfare between the Puritan who thought shame of revelation, and the artist who had to speak out, a battle never wholly won or lost, yet probably serving him well. For the inhibitions and reticences of the Dantesque or Puritan Frost have imposed on the sensuous singing Frost that austere and elegant poetical outline of

his. It is not as enigmatic as it seems to some of the
young intellectuals that he should have preferred
frugality to luxury in many realms of culture,
knowledge, and experience. His anti-æsthetic
prejudices, for instance, are essential to him. He
does not want superlatives. A rather bare world
suits him. His doubt of the trappings and self-
indulgences of the artist, which has in it more of
judgment than he usually allows himself (think
how little there is in his New England narratives,)
is a sort of armour to preserve his poetry intact.
He will not talk of art in his poetry except in
symbolic terms, as in "The Axe-helve," where he
endows a French workman with desires and aims
he can scarcely admit. And how deliberately he
makes his artistic ego the butt of his malice:

> I'm what is called a sensibilitist,
> Or otherwise an environmentalist;
> In other words, I know wherever I am,
> Being the creature of literature I am,
> I shall not lack for pains to keep me awake.

("Not so you'd notice it," appends a Frostian note
in pencil, "but still too much so for self-approval."
*Self-approval*—there the Puritan shows his spots.
The sensibility is, however, allowed.)

The satiric wrinkle that lifts the corner of his
long upper lip tells the whole story. In the heart
of his starkest tragedy we find the old New Eng-

land effort to compromise ideals and facts, escaping either in shy tenderness and beauty or in a whimsical humour that often verges on irony. Consider for tenderness "An Old Man's Winter Night"—one of Frost's ultimates in the union of form and substance; for humour "A Hundred Collars," and you will see that what looks like fancy is no more nor less than a fact. Yes, there is something strong and steady in Frost's spirit which takes account of his compromises, and holds the twisted strands of his life together for one central purpose. The claim one makes for him of first-rateness—he will make few claims for himself—rests in part on his sureness and continuity of poetic development. In life he has turned from one task to another, but in verse he has stuck with piety to the clarification of his own tone of voice, his own form and matter. If he is "Greek" it is not that he is truly pagan, but only that he has known how to choose from the world exactly what he needed for himself and his song—for himself as a singer.

One of the things he needed and found was a normal human destiny. Born in San Francisco; brought up from the age of ten by a mother and a grandfather in Lawrence, Massachusetts; looking in—no more—at Dartmouth College; he married young a very true New England girl—a marriage preserved like treasure through the years—retired to his rustic isolation of farming and teaching, and had in time four children, now launched in their own life paths. In all these level solitary seasons Frost was writing poetry with solid faith in his mission, though editors seemed to make little of it. When he stole away with his family on his decisive voyage to England in 1912, at the age of thirty-eight, the world where reputations are made was none the wiser, and he himself was far from conceiving that triumphant return two years later after the English publication of *A Boy's Will,* and *North of Boston.* Yet here were the editors drawn up on the dock, hailing him as a leader of his generation in the "new poetry"; here were rewards and successes which made farming somewhat vicarious and gave teaching a privileged academic form; here was leisure to produce *Mountain Interval* and *New Hampshire.* These books reveal that neither the "new poetry" nor the new opportunity have taken Frost farther from his native base than the stride to Michigan. You can find just one English poem—if you look hard: "The Sound of Trees." Frost recognized early that, like his Census-taker, he wanted life to go on living; but he has sought it where he stood.

The life he found, as revealed in his books, has a pattern, a colour, above all a sound, that must vanish like mist in the prose telling. Its background is a landscape, pearly in tone, lonely to those who do not recognize its friendliness; northern New England, broken in outline, with views but not giant views, mountains but not too high ones, pastures, swamps, farms deserted and farms occupied. This land, to the spare human figures who move across it, is an extension and explanation of themselves, as the Irish country to the fairy folk. And these New Englanders are somehow "folk" in addition to being real people and even local "characters." They are planted here by necessity, their roots are tangled in the roots of elm and cedar, their wisdom is all garnered from natural things. Those who find Frost's poetry sad and grey probably cannot bear the sheer clarity he gives to human lives in this thin northern atmosphere of his, shut in by a moral and physical solitude, yet escaping through their barriers to grapple together in situations of love and hate and suffering typical and inevitable of New England but also of "the world in general."

The landscape background is already sharply etched in *A Boy's Will,* that slender lyrical volume that gives off, through its changing subjective moods, a delicate aroma of young happiness, all mingled with the sensuous love of earth. The exile of Derry Farm, his shadowy reliant bride beside him, meets the seasons and their tasks alone, with no soul to interfere. Though one notes a few uncertainties which the older Frost has left be-

hind, here, already at his height, is the visual Frost,
Frost the "gloater"—"poetry is gloating"—who
has the power to look so hard at things that they
come to life—as in "The Vantage Point":

> My breathing shakes the bluet like a breeze,
>  I smell the earth, I smell the bruiséd plant,
> I look into the crater of the ant.

And here is Frost of the "concrete vocal image,"
already finding his own tones of speech—as in
"Mowing," the first "talk song" he was aware of,
or in "My November Guest." And Frost the arti-
ficer of tight and subtle verse form—in this respect he has never surpassed "Storm Fear":

> When the wind works against us in the dark,
> And pelts with snow
> The lower chamber window on the east,
> And whispers with a sort of stifled bark,
> The beast,
>               "Come out! Come out!"—
> It costs no inward struggle not to go,
> Ah, no!
> I count our strength,
> Two and a child,
> Those of us not asleep subdued to mark
> How the cold creeps as the fire dies at length,—
> How drifts are piled,
> Dooryard and road ungraded,
> Till even the comforting barn grows far away,
> And my heart owns a doubt
> Whether 'tis in us to arise with day
> And save ourselves unaided.

The book tells how a youth "was scared away from life and came back to it through a poem." The youth was "consumed with stars at fifteen, with flowers at twenty," as he tells elsewhere, "matter of history," and the poem was "The Tuft of Flowers":

> A leaping tongue of bloom the scythe had spared—

the scythe of an unknown reaper who thus restored Frost to his comradeship in the gregarious universe. On such fragilities do the lives of poets hang in literal fact. "Got me my first real job. Whole family owe their life to this poem and they'd better believe it."

"Mending Wall," the first poem in *North of Boston,* takes up the psychological theme where "A Tuft of Flowers" laid it down:

> Something there is that doesn't love a wall,
> That sends the frozen-ground-swell under it,
> And spills the upper boulders in the sun;
> And makes gaps even two can pass abreast.

Here is an older and more objective Frost, who has squarely accepted his human fate and seen himself for only a half-rustic, questioning, as he works on his side of the gaps, the true farmer's aphorism: "Good fences make good neighbours."

> My apple-trees will never get across
> And eat the cones under his pines, I tell him.

A characteristic accent, which would be recognizable at the Antipodes as Robert Frost. And how profoundly imagined the neighbour, symbol of a whole country race:

> Bringing a stone grasped firmly by the top
> In each hand, like an old stone savage armed.
> He moves in darkness as it seems to me,
> Not of woods only and the shade of trees.
> He will not go behind his father's saying,
> And he likes having thought of it so well
> He says again: "Good fences make good neighbours."

And so a conversation between two men about stone walls is really concerned with the life force, always building and breaking down, and serves as introduction to a book of searching human revelation.

The New England narratives in *North of Boston* established Frost's poetic majority. They were too fresh, mordant, unsentimental, to be read without a shock of recognition. Frost illumines character not by comment or explanation but through crisis. He is a dramatist rather than a story-teller. "Drama is all; a poem must create situation as much as a play"—and he lives up to it, even in a lyric of a butterfly. The diverse crises in marital relations summarized in "Home Burial," "The Death of the Hired Man," "The Housekeeper," "A Servant to Servants," might be dealt with at the pace of *Jude the Obscure*. Frost epit-

omizes them, without sacrificing that flavour of
talk which helps to give the poems their air of pastoral leisure. He has transformed blank verse into
a fluid instrument of his own idiomatic speech,
pungent and taciturn, a speech sharpened and
mellowed with a humour that strikes always
through its mark of literal fact. In these and the
similar narratives of people in later volumes the
verse is an element of the originality inherent
in spirit and structure alike. Another is Frost's
oblique method of dealing with grim realism.
However unescapable the horror—recall, for instance, the superb passage of "A Servant to Servants," where the woman who is losing her own
hold on reality tells how for her mother as a bride
"love things" were involved with the madness of
her husband's brother, in his cage in an upper
room—a tenderness as generic as sunshine, and as
uncritical, seems to play about the bitter truths.
In the same way the homespun background, the
bucolic detail, is transformed and sublimated by
a kind of abstract beauty and detachment, like
the abstract quality of Frost's sculptured head as
rendered in Du Chêne's fine bust, reproduced in
the books. If Virgil had been a plain dirt farmer
he could hardly have written the Eclogues. So
with Frost and his dramatic pastorals at Derry,
Franconia, and South Shaftesbury, Vermont.

The analogy with Virgil was made by Frost

himself. In my copy of the *Selected Poems*—a volume which should be more familiar to the public—he writes: " 'Black Cottage,' 'The House-keeper,' 'The Death of the Hired Man,' date from 1905" (his thirtieth year); "Virgil's Eclogues may have had something to do with them." And again, in the section containing "Mending Wall," "The Mountain," and other definitely pastoral poems: "First heard the voice from a printed page in a Virgilian Eclogue and *Hamlet*. Influenced by what I have supposed *Piers Plowman* to be. Never read it." To ladies who claim that they are "interested in the 'new poetry' but cannot understand it"—"That gives me a feeling in my arm, just in my arm!" Frost is likely to explain that Barnyard Verse goes back at least to the first poem in *The Oxford Book of English Verse*. He also enjoys the story of the agricultural college which pronounced "Good-Bye and Keep Cold"— a poem of an orchard—"pomologically accurate," while offering to amend the verse. His irony would spurn any over-estimation of "influences." Yet consider the opening of "The Mountain":

> The mountain held the town as in a shadow.
> I saw so much before I slept there once:
> I noticed that I missed stars in the west,
> Where its black body cut into the sky.
> Near me it seemed: I felt it like a wall
> Behind which I was sheltered from a wind.

Here is a spacious mood established in a few lines, a love relation predicated between a man and a mountain; and as the rhythmic pattern unfolds, the reader is transplanted into a realm of brooding tranquillity. The poem was written "with one stroke of the pen," as were three other favourites from the later volumes—Frost hopes one day to publish the four together—"Birches," "Two Look at Two," and that perfect lyric, "Stopping by Woods on a Snowy Evening." In all the same exquisite inter-transfusion between man and nature, the same allusiveness which starts long whispering echoes in the mind and heart, the same cherishing of an objective image in a poet's dream and fantasy until it is ready to flow out upon the page at last in calm and eternal shape.

Let those who will debate Frost's place in the old poetry or the new: what makes him, as I believe, one of the few authentic poets of his age is that he is (as I began by saying) a star-gazer, who writes for the satisfaction of his own curiosity. Every poem is a fresh discovery. The general shape of his curiosity was fixed in those first two volumes. Frost has not tried to change it—indeed he has tried not to, since the aim of an artist, to him, is the "undrossing" of himself. *Mountain Interval* and *New Hampshire* are not pioneering but fulfilment; they extract new and rich treasure from known veins of ore, lyrical and narrative, as the poet's life has been enriched and eased but not basically altered by success and geniality. Greater preoccupation with the vocal side of verse we do find: here Frost intuitively feels himself to be most himself. To translate the actual shape and sound of living speech into poetry is the chief aim of his prime.

All the fun is how you say a thing.

Comment: "And the chance it gives you for tones of voice."

Frost is theorizing about poetry. See him stretched out in the sweet-fern, under a bountiful August sun, eyes and shirt coloured like juniper, hair shaded like grey bark, eyebrows of a rogue, lips of a caustic wit. He is soliloquizing to one of those projections of his wandering self—maybe the Gum-gatherer.

They call me a New England dialect poet. . . . Not so you'd notice it. It was never my aim to keep to any special speech unliterary, vernacular or slang. I lay down no law to myself there. What I have been after from the first, consciously and unconsciously, is tones of voice. I've wanted to write down certain brute throat noises so that no one could miss them in my sentences. I have been guilty of speaking of sentences as a mere notation for indicating them. I have counted on doubling the meaning of my sentences with them. They have been my observation and my subject-matter.

I know what I want to do most. I don't do it often enough. In "The Runaway" I added the moral at the end

301

just for the pleasure of the aggrieved tone of voice. There are high spots in respect of vocal image in "Blueberries":

> There *had* been some berries—but those were all gone.
> He didn't say where they had been. He went on:
> "I'm sure—I'm sure"—as polite as could be.

Frost the shrewd, lounging rascal, has vanished behind the junipers. In his place I fancy I see an austere, hieratical figure, serving a rustic altar with a ritual of his own making. And these are some of the ritualistic words:

> Imagery and after-imagery are about all there is to poetry. Synecdoche and synecdoche—— My motto is that something has to be left to God.

> In making a poem you have no right to think of anything but the subject-matter. After making it, no right to boast of anything but the form.

> A poem must at least be as good as the prose it might have been. A poem is a box with a *set* or assortment of sentences that just fit together to fill it. You are rhyming sentences and phrases, not just words. They must go into it as unchanged in size and shape as the words.

> A straight crookedness is most to be desired in a stick or a line. Or a crooked straightness. An absolutely abandoned zigzag that goes straight to the mark.

See him standing on his hill-top, this Virgilian who, for all his crooked, New England speech has made the ancient renunciation, and for all his love of earth left earth behind. Remember "Into My Own," the first poem in *A Boy's Will,* which is also the last in the *Selected Poems:*

> One of my wishes is that those dark trees,
> So old and firm they scarcely show the breeze,
> Were not, as 'twere, the merest mask of gloom,
> But stretched away unto the edge of doom.
>
> I should not be withheld but that some day
> Into their vastness I should steal away,
> Fearless of ever finding open land,
> Or highway where the slow wheel pours the sand.
>
> I do not see why I should e'er turn back. . . .

Against this Robert Frost has written: "This began it. *Exeo.*"

# CHAPTER XV

# OLIVER WENDELL HOLMES

*Justice Touched with Fire*

OLIVER WENDELL HOLMES

*Camera Portrait by E. O. Hoppé*

# OLIVER WENDELL HOLMES

*Justice Touched with Fire*

ERE is a Yankee, strayed from Olympus. Olympians are reputed at ease in the universe; they know truth in flashes of fire, and reveal its immortal essence in cryptic phrase. How disturbing to the solemnities of average mortals, average lawyers, average judges even, is the swift, searching, epigrammatic thought of Mr. Justice Holmes. Even the wise-cracks he loves to fling out are keyed to profundity and wit. He has lived through the most restless periods of American history since the American Revolution itself, yet his early divinations of the law, outlined nearly half a century ago, and his Supreme Court opinions, which have together recast American legal thinking, seem to have been formulated in the elegant leisure that we associate with the classics.

Oliver Wendell Holmes's tall and erect figure, which a ripe and white old age has scarcely stooped; his grand manner, at once noble and dazzling—those have never asked quarter of time. Watch his snowy head for a moment among his younger peers on the bench. Note the set of the shoulders in the gown, the oval contour of the face with its fine, angular New England features, the flow of the level white brows into the thin distinction of the nose, the martial mustachios, with their heavy guardsman's droop and their curved ends of punctilio. The eyes, the most striking feature, give off sparkles of scintillating grey-blue, and have more scepticism and gentle malice than mercy in their depths. Though at bottom Holmes is and looks a simple American gentleman of aristocratic rectitude, he has a spice of the Mephistophelean quality which he himself has recommended to the naïveté of judges.

The Justice is listening to a complex argument —listening till his mind, hovering and intent, like the wasp that paralyses the caterpillar, has driven straight to its heart. Then, while the other judges still patiently listen, he reads over the briefs, calls the pages to bring reports containing opinions relied on by counsel, and is ready, by the time counsel is rising to his peroration, to draft an opinion that will not fail to "strike the jugular."

The jurist who, at fourscore years and five, can command this penetration of essentials, this intense focusing of mental powers, has some rare elixir in his veins. Is it not the true elixir of youth? The youth offered by a young Bostonian to his country in the most heroic of her wars, and thrice wounded, at Ball's Bluff, Antietam, and Fredericksburg? Judge Holmes's clearest genius—the sharp and supple functioning of his mind—in some nameless fashion draws its strength from his curiosity and awe in the face of the mystery of existence. It seems that the near presence of death in those three stern and shadowed years fused his intellect and his emotion in a single shaft of will. It made sceptical philosophy a necessity, but gave to fundamental doubt a practical idealism. It affirmed man's destiny on earth as battle, his chances those of war. But it discovered to him that the root of joy as of duty and the worth of life itself is to put out all one's powers to the full, though the end be dim and the plan of campaign little understood. "Men carry their signatures upon their persons," he has written, "although they may not always be visible at the first glance." The friends of the Justice all know the signature that the Civil War inscribed. It is that of a youthful fighter who somehow inspired the fate of the lonely thinker with the faith of the soldier.

THE son of Dr. Oliver Wendell Holmes was a fortunate youth. Born in the flower of New England's cultural dominance, and at the dawn of the

Darwinian age into a family at once brahminical, literary, and scientific, brought up at that
"autocratic" breakfast-table where a bright saying gave a child a double help of marmalade, he
must early have acquired the rich flavour of belles-
lettres which in him has ever mellowed the scientific habit. Celebrated men were familiars at his
father's house, and from the greatest among them
—Emerson—he drew a priceless intellectual ferment. Yet, with his glancing wit and his worldly
charm, he might have been tempted away from
the isolated path of the original thinker but for
the war of secession. It was, in his own view, his
greatest good fortune to graduate from Harvard
in the class of '61, at the age of twenty, just as
this war was beginning, and to learn one day, as
he was walking down Beacon Hill, with Hobbes's
*Leviathan* in his hand, that he had a commission
in the Twentieth Massachusetts Volunteers; a
regiment commemorated at last in the Boston
Public Library by one of the lions of St. Gaudens
that guard the entrance stairway. So the young
officer, whom we may see in his uniform at Lang-
dell Hall, at the Harvard Law School, with his
visored cap on his knee, in one of those touching
little faded photographs which were a sop to pa-
rental love—a mere lad, trusting and vulnerable,
like all lads who have fought all the great wars—

went forth to a baptism that he has never forgotten.

It came at Ball's Bluff: an engagement where
the Twentieth Massachusetts got its first crucial
trial. There were tactical errors which cost dear.
The blues, defeated but "too proud to surrender,"
as the greys declared, were driven down the cliff
on the Virginia shore into the Potomac, where,
dying, swimming, drowning in numbers, they yet
struggled to transport the survivors and the
wounded in the few sinking boats to the island in
mid-stream, and then to the Maryland shore,
while the river was whipped into a foam of bul-
lets, and darkness fell. Lieutenant Holmes, ap-
parently mortally wounded in the breast, was laid
in a boat with dying men and ferried through
the night. As he recovered consciousness, he heard
the man next him groan and—thinking he probably had his own dose—said to himself:

"I suppose Sir Philip Sidney would say: 'Put
that man ashore first.' I think I will let events
take their course."

A story written down by the elder Holmes in
the *Atlantic Monthly* (not altogether to the pleasure of the younger?) is indicative of another side
of the Justice's character. This relates how, after
the battle of Antietam, Dr. Holmes started out to
search for a wounded son. But the doctor could

not find his young hero, though he followed this clue and that. At last, in despair, he was taking a train for the north at Hagerstown, Maryland, when, "in the first car, on the fourth seat to the right, I saw my captain."

"Hullo, my boy!"

"Boy, nothing!" (The original tale does not run quite this way.) The "boy" had been spending a week much to his taste. "As he walked languidly along [in Hagerstown], some ladies saw him across the street and, seeing, were moved with pity and, pitying, spoke such soft words that he was tempted to accept their invitation to rest awhile beneath their hospitable roof. The mansion was old, as the dwellings of gentlefolk should be; the ladies were some of them young, and all were full of kindness; there were gentle cares and unasked luxuries and pleasant talk, and music sprinklings for the piano, with a sweet voice to keep them company."

The words call up, along with other images of an America gone for ever, a quaint photograph found in a portfolio in the Memorial Alcove at the Boston Library: a bevy of devout young ladies in bustles and tight waists and long, flowing skirts, sewing together on a flag. Such a flag was presented, after Ball's Bluff, to Company E "by the sisters of Lieutenants Lowell and Putnam," with a polished letter from Charles Eliot Norton about the honour of the Bay State. The Colonel of the Twentieth, by the way, on first reaching head-quarters, and asked by the commanding officer if he had arms, uniforms, and accoutrements, re-plied proudly: "My regiment, sir, came from Massachusetts."

Back to Massachusetts, then, came young Holmes, to the soil for whose outcropping rocks and barberry bushes and sand dunes and old towns built of brick and shingle he has confessed a rooted affection. He had no path to blaze unless he chose: the natural Puritan aristocracy from which he sprang awaited him with its pleasant securities. But there burned in this young man, as there burns in the Holmes of to-day, a sense of the valuable brevity of existence. Life was a rich but a responsible adventure, and he had a simple dem-ocratic conviction, denied to some who are born under the shadow of Beacon Hill, that "the deep-est cause we have to love our country" is "that instinct, that spark, that makes the American un-able to meet his fellow man otherwise than simply as a man, eye to eye, hand to hand, and foot to foot, wrestling naked on the sand." Holmes was recognizing fiery energies which later claimed mountain climbing as an outlet. A stern intellec-tual ambition, worthy substitute for the primitive and heroic, was taking shape. A sentence of his own conjures him up for me, standing apart even in his tested group: "In our youth our hearts were touched with fire. It was given to us to learn at the outset that life is a profound and passionate thing."

It is hinted that among those young ladies of the best families who—Boston being truly a village in the sixties—"knew every carriage in town," the return of a handsome wounded soldier (also the class poet of the decimated '61) made a stir. "That lanky talker of a Wendell Holmes" was an old maid-servant's dictum. Holmes has always loved talking by a fire with a clever and gracious woman, and these ghostly maidens, if they yet lived, could probably tell us why a young man of varied and brilliant parts chose from several possible destinies to enter the Harvard Law School.

For there was also literature, there was above all philosophy. Holmes was not the man to follow in his father's footsteps, or even in Emerson's, though he had in fact qualities as a literary stylist far superior to the doctor's, and gifts as a philosopher which gave a universal impress to his legal thinking. The winds and waves of eternity beat through his writings. "Nerve and dagger," said Emerson, are lacking in the American genius. Holmes the writer has nerve and dagger, as he has in moral and intellectual issues a blade-like courage. But he did not dream, in those tormented days, of being named among great American writers and philosophers. In his twenties this profession of the law which he had elected seemed barren enough. Did he choose it, by a quirk common to New Englanders, for that very reason? Because it was hard, male, undesired? The law enforced more than thought: an activity in the world of men, a reality which the soldier felt bound to espouse, if only that it was so alien to his intuitive bent for inward brooding thought. "It cost me some years of doubt and unhappiness," the Justice has avowed, "before I could say to myself: 'The law is part of the universe—if the universe can be thought about, one part must reveal it as much as another to one who can see that part. It is only a question if you have the eyes.'"

THE study of philosophy helped Holmes to find his legal eyes. He likes to tell how he began to read Plato, as an undergraduate at Harvard, and was admonished by Emerson: "Hold him at arm's length. You must say to yourself: 'Plato, you have pleased the world for two thousand years: let us see if you can please me.'" The sequel is pertinent. Young Holmes not only read, but turned off a critical essay which he showed expectantly to his mentor. "I have read your piece. When you strike at a king, you must *kill* him." That shaft went

straight to the bull's eye. When Holmes graduated
from the Law School he approached his profession
in the spirit of scientific and philosophic inquiry.
Not as do the practitioners "to whom the law is
a rag-bag from which they pick out the piece and
the colour that they want." Holmes had no con-
suming interest in practice, considered as winning
cases and making money. But he had the hope, as
yet scarce conscious, of shooting with true aim at
some great intellectual marks. "I suppose the law
is worthy of the interest of an intelligent man,"
he once hazarded, in his anguish of doubt whether
it was, to Charles Francis Adams, the Minister to
England.

That a philosopher could be, must be, a man of
intelligence Holmes was morally certain. Was he
not "twisting the tail of the cosmos" with his
friend Bill James? One gets from the early letters
of William James a fine series of images of two
golden and impetuous youths, whetting thought
on thought, doubt on doubt, in an upper chamber.
In the year 1866, when "Bill" was twenty-four
and studying medicine, and "Wendle" twenty-
five and studying law, they exchanged acute argument on materialism. A year later, when James
had gone to Germany to pursue philosophy, and
Holmes had been admitted to the bar, discussions
of "our dilapidated old friend the Kosmos" continued by letter—interspersed by affectionate

reminiscence from James, of "your whitely lit-up room, drinking in your profound wisdom, your golden jibes, your costly imagery, listening to your shuddering laughter." "Why don't you join the Society for Psychical Research?" James is said to have inquired. To which Holmes: "Why don't you investigate Mohammedanism? There are millions of men who think you will be damned without it. Life is like an artichoke, you pull out a leaf, a tip only is edible. You pull out a day, only an hour or two is available for spiritual thoughts."

Holmes was looking, though he may not have realized it, for a personal philosophy that he could use as a raft from which to take the long, deep plunge into his legal-scholarly pursuits. It is typical—for his power of choice and exclusion, his economy of time and means are facets of his greatness—that he did not continue to flounder about in the philosophic waters, trying this system and that, cursing Jehovah and calling on his angels to save, but grasped the planks that he found near at hand and skilfully fitted them together into the aforementioned raft. *Raft* is too perishable a word. Holmes's philosophy was a tidy boat, formed, for all its pointed nails of scepticism, of sturdy Puritan oak, a shipshape bark, in which he could cruise safely about the cosmos among the other worlds and the stars.

Every speech, every personal letter, every opinion of Oliver Wendell Holmes rests on this hardy and lucid doctrine. Divergent though it was from the philosophy of James—who continued his search for a solution that would fit the fate of Man in general, and for himself tended toward those supernatural revelations and consolations which Holmes's scepticism impatiently repudiated,—the affectionate relation continued through life. And every distant interchange made the old philosophic quarrel flare up. The following statement of Holmes's "platform,"—happily preserved in the James files—though written from the Supreme Court in 1901, "after reading your two pieces about Pragmatism (pedantic name)" might as well have been written in 1875, or, if William James had lived, in 1926.

"It is as absurd" (the Justice remarks, with familiar humility, before an expert) "for me to be spearing my old commonplaces at you as it would be for an outsider to instruct me in the theory of legal responsibility—but you see, *mon vieux,* although it is years since we have had any real talk together, I am rather obstinate in my adherence to ancient sympathies and enjoy letting out a little slack to you."

"I have been in the habit of saying that all I mean by truth is what I can't help thinking. The assumption of the validity of the thinking process seems to mean no more than that. But I have learned to surmise that my *can't helps* are not necessarily cosmic . . . philosophy seems to me generally speaking to sin through arrogance . . . I can't help preferring champagne to ditch water, but I doubt if the uni-

verse does. . . . The great act of faith is when a man de-
cides that he is not God. . . . If I did come out of it [the
universe] or rather if I am in it, I see no wonder that I can't
swallow it. If it fixed my bounds, as it gives me my powers,
I have nothing to say about its possibilities or characteristics,
except that it is the kind of a thing (using this phraseology
sceptically and under protest) that has me in its belly and so
is bigger than I. It seems to me that my only promising activity is to make *my* universe coherent and livable, not to
babble about *the* universe."

THESE passages define a consistent character.
Judge Holmes has, at eighty-five, an intellectual
youth that most men of forty cannot boast. He
lives greatly in the brilliant young legal minds of
to-day; believes that there are more men of promise in the present than in his own youth; receives
their ideas with the courtesy, admiration, and
speculative curiosity accorded to honoured guests.
One of his favourite aphorisms is that the average
life of an idea is fifteen years; another, that the
literature of the past is a bore. Yet it is to be
noted (since the laity persist in labelling him a
radical) that, though he admires Proust and finds
*Nize Baby* richly droll, he is more often to be seen,
in that dignified Washington study of his, with a
volume of eighteenth-century memoirs in his
hand than with a daily newspaper. His own universe, material, spiritual, or intellectual, is not
subject to perpetual revision. His economics, like
his philosophy and his literary tastes, were pretty

well settled in the twenties. The foundations of his legal thinking were laid in the thirties. His domestic happiness, which continues unbroken to this day, was established at the age of thirty-one—fifty-four years ago.

Meanwhile he was taking his plunge into the deep waters of the law. In 1869 James comments that "Wendell" is working too hard, taking no vacation. In 1870 he assumes the editorship of the *American Law Review*. In 1873 appears his important edition of Kent's *Commentaries,* and in the same year he becomes a member of the firm of Shattuck, Holmes and Munroe. But he cannot have given much time to practice, for the years from thirty to forty were a period of intensive research: a time of lonely and original productivity, often hinted at in his speeches, when he learned "to lay his course by a star which he has never seen"; and, feeling around him "a black gulf of solitude more isolating than that which surrounds the dying man," learned also to trust his "own unshaken will." During these years he offered his life to the law as completely as he had offered it to his country; and, losing it, found it again in his classic *Common Law,* which dates an epoch in American legal history.

The chapters were written first, as a Boston classic should be, in the form of "Lowell Lectures," and delivered in 1880. Published as a learned volume in 1881, the book was hailed by those competent to judge, both in America and in England, as a great and even a prophetic work. "The law embodies the story of a nation's development through the centuries," we read at the outset, "and it cannot be dealt with as if it contained only the axioms and corollaries of a book of mathematics." "The life of the law has not been logic; it has been experience." Together with the legal essays published before and after in the journals of the period, the book established, as Dean Pound has pointed out, that "functional" and relative view of the law now generally accepted as replacing the anatomical and morphological. Jurisprudence had been considered a self-sufficient science, with traditions all but God-given. Holmes discovered, by following a "right" or some other legal symbol to its early source, that the tradition was based often on some unreasoned survival that had lost all meaning. "The common law"—the phrase, from a later opinion, is famous—"is not a brooding omnipresence in the sky." Holmes emphasized the need of "thinking things rather than words." Pound says that he anticipated the teachers of to-day by thirty years or more. "The Epigoni could easily forget whose armour they were wearing and whose weapons they were wielding."

Justice Holmes's career as a jurist covers eras of rapid and organic social change and his eminence owes much to the insight—an insight very different from the piling of fact on fact—with which he has held the balance between history, experience, and timely necessity. He scrutinized the historical texts not for antiquarian reasons, not to discover an absolute—for in law, as in philosophy, he knew that he was not God—but for a concrete revelation of "man's destiny upon this earth." And looking back, he began to see the law at last as his constant and all-inclusive mistress: "A princess mightier than she who once wrought at Bayeux, eternally weaving into her web dim figures out of the ever lengthening past . . . disclosing every painful step and every world-shaking contest by which mankind has worked and fought its way from savage isolation to organic social life."

The fame that resulted from *The Common Law* led to a professorship at the Harvard Law School, and before the same year, 1882, was out, to an appointment to the Massachusetts Supreme Bench— "a stroke of lightning which changed all the course of my life." On this bench Holmes spent twenty fertile years, Associate Justice till 1899, Chief Justice till 1902. He managed his court with a practised hand. But through these Boston years, as now, he wore an air of detachment which marked him, in his native town, with a kind of uncommonness, and so, in certain quarters, with a kind of suspicion. The "village" never queries its failures: Tom Blank is a queer duck, but he is the son of John Blank, the banker. Now Oliver Wendell Holmes, Jr., was never the son of the doctor. He was a peacock with shining plumage; he flew afield and consorted with famous English jurists, like Bryce and Sir Frederick Pollock. He climbed Alps with Leslie Stephen. He enjoyed free spirits, whether Back Bay brahmins, or Jews, or Roman Catholic priests. He invited a labour leader to his home. (Said the man: "You have changed my feeling. I used to see an enemy in every house.") With women he had the ease and gaiety of a Parisian or a Viennese, and sought their company. He was impatient with dullness and long-windedness, suggesting, when Chief Justice, that the lawyers of the state would greatly oblige him by taking a course in risqué French novels and so learn to speak in innuendo rather than at length. Yet, all the while, he was more absorbed by the discoveries of his own mind than by the privileges or limitations of the world about him. The mind accompanied his tall and elegant figure, in Boston as elsewhere, a pervasive and sceptical presence at every feast.

At a dinner given by the Boston Bar Association two years before the nomination of Oliver

Wendell Holmes by Roosevelt to the Supreme Bench of the United States, the Chief Justice, in his responsive speech, asked himself what he had to show for this half lifetime that had passed—"I look into my book, in which I keep a docket of the decisions . . . which fall to me to write, and find about a thousand cases, many of them upon trifling or transitory matters . . . a thousand cases, when one would have liked to study to the bottom and to say his say on every question which the law ever presented. . . . We are lucky enough if we can give a sample of our best and if in our hearts we can feel that it has been nobly done."

This reads like a peroration: it was a prelude to the richest maturity of Holmes's life. Twenty-five more years on the Supreme Bench, a thousand more cases, and the Justice still on the firing line. Nearly half a century altogether that Holmes has been "living through," as judge, the wisdom whose foundations were laid before forty. The phrase is his partner, Shattuck's, spoken in a moment when it seemed to Holmes, after many honours, that he had tasted the full feast of the law: "Now you must live it through." One may relate the words to a comment of Dean Wigmore that Justice Holmes is the only one of the long list of judges of the American Supreme Courts who framed for himself a system of legal truths and general truths of life, and composed his opinions in harmony with the system.

The system was flexible because at bottom it was an attitude of tolerance based on insight into the complexity of human affairs. It has done more than any system of orthodoxies to make the Supreme Court a tribunal, as Professor Felix Frankfurter has said, where inevitable frictions between the individual and society, between the expanding powers of the states and nation could be fought out, instead of a deistic chamber operating by scholastic formulæ. Holmes's wish has been ever to harmonize conflicting interests; to see where man's social desires come from, and where they are tending. (He maintains that the "little decisions" frequently reveal more of interstitial change in the tissue of the law than famous disputes about a telephone company.) Though he proceeds from the general to the particular, he repudiates finalities. Behind his generalizations are intuitions of reality.

Minority decisions have probably made Mr. Justice Holmes's reputation with the rank and file. Yet his famous dissents as well as his majority decisions have frequently run counter to his personal prejudice. "The decision of a gentleman," says a Boston friend. The decision of a poet would be equally true. For to Holmes a fire smoulders at the core of things which makes them for ever plastic and mobile. *Plus ça change, plus c'est la même chose,* says the French sceptic. Holmes feels that the universe may be "too great a swell to condescend to have a meaning," but he is bound to accept the temporary pattern. "The best test of truth is the power of the thought to get itself accepted in the competition of the market. . . . Every year, if not every day, we have to wager our salvation upon some prophecy based upon imperfect knowledge." The Justice never refuses such a wager, but, taking it up, he uses his mind as guide rather than as dictator. His conservative critics cannot point to a single self-interested opinion. His best friends cannot boast that he has ever decided things their way. Indeed, President Roosevelt, who appointed him because he imagined Holmes had "the right ideas"—i. e., T. R.'s— soon was taught a lesson in true judicial-mindedness by Holmes's dissent in Roosevelt's pet case against the Northern Securities merger.

Roosevelt used to urge young men to fight for *their* ideas. So did President Eliot, whose prejudices were the defect of his passion. Holmes the sceptic thinks one idea very like another, but Holmes the New Englander knows well the difference between one aim and another. So his counsel to young lawyers is: Do the handsome thing, young feller! Don't be content to be a lawyer, be

a lawyer in the grand manner. If you are sailing
an intellectual bark, prepare for rigours, and head
for the Pole. Forget subjectivities, be a willing
instrument. Wreak yourself upon life. "If you
want to hit a bird on the wing, you must have all
your will in a focus. . . . Every achievement is
a bird on the wing." Key sentences which reveal
a freedom from passion that has made the ideal
judicial temper.

A JUDGE of the Federal bench tells of driving
with Justice Holmes to the Capitol one morning
some years ago, in that neat brougham drawn
by a fat cob, with a highly respectable coloured
coachman on the box, in which Holmes used to
be recognized on the Washington streets. The
Justice had got out of the carriage and was strid-
ing off, vigorous and loose-limbed, toward the
dome when the younger man called out humorously: "Do justice, sir!" Holmes wheeled: "Come
here, young feller!" and then, "I am not here to
do justice. I am here to play the game according
to the rules. When I was at the bar and Lowell
used to beat, I'd say to him: 'Judge, your result
may be good, but it's another game I undertook to
play. I gave you a thrust in tierce and you coun-
tered with a bag of potatoes over my head.' "

When in some summer hour of ease in his home
at Beverly Farms on the Massachusetts shore—an

unpretentious Victorian house, with a gravel drive and formal flower-beds set with cannas and geraniums—he turns to Pepys's *Diary*—"this and Walpole's *Letters* are the two books if you don't want ideas, and don't want to waste your time"— he looks misty at the duel of two friends who fought for love. When he finds himself in the dentist's chair he recalls that fear of pain and rattling musketry which only the brave admit preceded the attack. His intimate talk still breaks into Civil War slang—"Shut your trap!"—his speeches and letters are full of war metaphors and allusions to this past which he says he "cannot bear to read about," perhaps because his remembered picture is too final to bear the intervention of historians, who describe how Sherman kept Lincoln waiting, and why great battles failed. Writing to Henry James, he is "firing away at high pressure with breech-loading speed." In a speech: "When once the dead fifers of thirty years since begin to play in my head, the laws are silent." In another: "Life is a roar of bargain and battle, but in the very heart of it there rises a mystical spiritual tone. . . . It transmutes the dull details into romance. It reminds us that our only but wholly adequate significance is as parts of the unimaginable whole."

This seasoned judge, this gallant gentleman of the old New England, is the most romantic of contemporary Americans. He starts off for the court every morning at 11.30 as if on an errand for the gods—whereas he is to listen to argument from 12.00 to 2.00; lunch from 2.00 to 2.30; sit again from 2.30 to 4.30. Judge Cardozo has used, of his sentences, the word *phosphorescence.* Always Holmes gives out light. When he returns from the court to the sober dignity of his old house on I Street—formerly it was on foot; now the Chief Justice is likely to drive him a part of the distance; but who can be sure that, disdaining his elevator, he will not still take his stairs two steps at a time?—he will be able, with the young secretary who guards the book-lined antechamber of his library, with the visitor, to search thought and make it glow. The secretary—a new jewel of the Harvard Law School every year—wears an exalted air. He must promise not to get engaged during the period. "But I reserve the right," says the Justice with a twinkle, "to die or resign." With this young mind the Justice twists the tail of the still recalcitrant cosmos, engages in legal disputation, reads his opinions for criticism as modestly as if he were a novice. Sometimes, but rarely, there is a point of law to look up. For Holmes carries the law in his head, as a prophet the words of the Lord. And the Justice, in his own fine and ornamental script, answers every personal letter scrupulously, almost within the hour. "My messenger is waiting." Off it goes. The eye that falls upon the delicate missive in the cheap plethora of the morning mail has found treasure. Every page has some metaphysical touchstone, some literary epigram or casual heresy. "I must read *Twelfth Night* once more—a little girl tells me Shakspere is long in getting to the point. I think we take ourselves too seriously."

Mr. Justice Holmes, who has permanently enriched our law, our literature, our philosophy— of whom another distinguished judge has said: "There is Holmes—and there are all the other judges"—takes himself far less seriously than any good Rotarian. That blithe nonchalance, that true humbleness in the face of acknowledged human vanities, seems to his friends a part of his unerring taste. But it provokes distrust in those who need the support of the rolling platitudes of the Fathers. Holmes bears his critics no grudge. His courtesy to his fellows, like his generosity, is basic, and he has an innocent heart. When one sees his gracious figure outlined against his bookshelves full of classics, with their spaces for the books the Lord will omit mentioning, and their gaps for the books of the future, one is struck by its unquenchable youth. The face has a fine fresh colour, the voice, with its humorous vain echo of hesitation— mmm—that seems to set off the sparks in the eyes, has clarity and fervour. Maliciously it expunges the name of a popular New England poet from the slate of time, honestly it admits that gentlemen prefer blondes. But it will never allow our modern American idol, publicity, a niche in this hospitable library. If glory is here, she is hidden, diffused into a clear serenity, a scent of tender memory, a vital intellectual replenishment.

Yet do not think of Oliver Wendell Holmes as meagrely recompensed. He has found it well, he says, to have philosophy "the main wind of his life blowing from the side, instead of from behind." He has had his reward in the inspired performance of a daily task, in the constant siege of the eternal verities. Holmes was an infantry officer, at Ball's Bluff, but in the field of ideas he belongs to an arm more mobile. I see him as a light horseman, a fabulous skirmisher, a cavalier for all his "cold Puritan passion," who carries a pennon as well as a lance, and with it "that little flutter which means ideals."